Christmas 2000

Dear Lisa,
 merry Christmas!
Here's to many
Romantic, And Delicious
Dinners in 2001
And Always!
 Love, Barb

"Take the moment
let it happen,
hug the moment
make it last."

"DO I HEAR A WALTZ"
by STEVEN SONDHEIM and
RICHARD ROGERS, 1965

A TUSCAN SEDUCTION

A ROMANTIC COOKBOOK FOR TWO by JAMES LAMBETH and MILES JAMES

To Joyce and Courtney,
the loves of our lives.

A TUSCAN SEDUCTION
A ROMANTIC COOKBOOK FOR TWO
by JAMES LAMBETH and MILES JAMES

MIAMI DOG PRESS, JOHNSON, ARKANSAS, U.S.A.

MIAMI DOG PRESS, INC, 3906 Greathouse
Springs Road, Post Office Box 409, Johnson,
Arkansas 72741 Tel. 501-521-1304/Toll Free 888-
289-7090, Fax.501-521-8091, MIAMIDOG @AOL.COM

Book design and photography by James
Lambeth, FAIA, FAAR Food design, prepa-
ration and recipes by Chef Miles James
Computer Graphics and Typography by
Wendy Lott, Bella Vista, AR. and Lee Holt
of Collier's Photo Digital of Fayetteville, AR

Library of Congress Cataloging-in-Publication Data

Lambeth, James, 1942-
   A Tuscan seduction : a romantic cookbook for two / by
James Lambeth and Miles James.
     p. cm.
   Includes bibliographical references and index.
   ISBN 0-9601678-6-2 (case ; alk. paper)
   1. Cookery, Italian--Tuscan style. 2. Cookery for two.
   I. James, Miles, 1968- II. Title.

TX723.2.T86 L36 2000
641.5945'5--dc21
                              00-030505

Stainless serving pieces used in food pho-
tographs designed by Rangthong™ from
Thai Home Industries of Bangkok, Thailand.

First edition, 2000, printed in Canada by D.W.
Friesens, Printers through Four Color Imports, Ltd.

Imagine the arrival of the unique fruits and vegetables from the New World . . . from the place they called the Americas. The new foods were brought by Columbus. . . capsicum peppers, both sweet and hot, both crimson and gold. And there was corn and tomatoes and new colorful beans and squash . . . they might as well have come from a another planet.

How exciting it must have been in Florence at that wondrous time. The spoiled children of the Medici laughing and running though the vegetable carts of the Mercato Vecchio, bumping against a young Michelangelo, or Botticelli, or DaVinci, or the shy one they called Machiavelli.

The Renaissance of Tuscan food was mirrored by the incredible exuberance of the new art and architecture of this great Italian Renaissance. . . one feeding the other. . . each glittering in the light of the birth of the 16th century.

And now, in our time, almost a half millennium later, we still make pilgrimages to Tuscany - to feel and see and taste the place that shaped our daily lives. To walk through the same spaces, listen to the same music, and taste the same cuisine that altered Western Civilization. That is the Tuscan seduction.

This cookbook records our Tuscan experience through the eyes of an American architect and an American chef. We traveled through the seasons from the winter to summer. . . from a rare snowfall in the central hill towns to the beaches of the western boundaries.

As the climate and geography changes in Tuscany, so too does the cuisine. From hearty winter dishes to the fresh vegetables of spring and summer. The ingredients also change with the region. . . with wild boar, pheasant, and rabbit from the northern forests, the vineyards and olive groves of the central rolling hills, and the seafood from the islands of the Tyrrhenian Sea.

Our hope is that you too will be seduced by Tuscany as we have been. We have included recipes and menus that should set the stage for many romantic feasts for two. They are easy to prepare and possess a beauty that is unique to Tuscany.

We invite you to play your favorite Andrea Bocelli recording, pour yourself and your love luscious glasses of Chianti Classico Riserva, and let the seduction begin.

". . . kisses, licks, bites, thrusts, and stings."

DESCRIPTION OF TUSCAN WINE by
MICHELANGELO, 1503

WINTER

TABLE OF CONTENTS

• WINTER •

• SUMMER •

TABLE OF CONTENTS

• ALL OF THE RECIPES AND MENUS ARE GENEROUS PORTIONS FOR TWO •

"I'll feel as I felt with her,
wed to her and weightless,
caught as if by a dance."

INTERVIEW WITH THE VAMPIRE by ANNE RICE, 1976

MONTEPULCIANO MENU

Fagioli con olio d'olive, erbe e pepe
TUSCAN WHITE BEANS WITH OLIVE OIL, HERBS AND BLACK PEPPER

Pici con pepe, parmigiano ed olio
PICI WITH BLACK PEPPER, PARMESAN AND OLIVE OIL

Coniglio alla contadina
PEASANT STYLE BRAISED RABBIT

Fagioli con olio d'olive, erbe e pepe
TUSCAN WHITE BEANS WITH OLIVE OIL, HERBS AND BLACK PEPPER

Pici con pepe, parmigiano ed olio
PICI WITH BLACK PEPPER, PARMESAN AND OLIVE OIL

Coniglio alla contadina
PEASANT STYLE BRAISED RABBIT

Fagioli con olio d'olive, erbe e pepe

TUSCAN WHITE BEANS WITH OLIVE OIL, HERBS AND BLACK PEPPER

Ingredients

1/2 pound white beans

Fresh chopped herbs

Salt and black pepper

Olive oil

Method

In a bowl, cover the white beans with cold water and soak for 12 hours. Once the beans are soaked, in a heavy-bottomed pot bring 8 cups of water to the boil. Add 2 tablespoons of salt to the boiling water and add the soaked beans. Bring the beans back to the boil and turn down to a simmer. Cook the beans for 35 to 40 minutes or until tender throughout. Remove the beans from the heat and drain. Place the beans in a mixing bowl and add the herbs, olive oil and salt and pepper. Allow to cool to room temperature and serve.

Pici con pepe, parmigiano ed olio

PICI WITH BLACK PEPPER, OLIVE OIL AND PARMESAN

Ingredients

1 pound Pici pasta

Salt and black pepper

Olive oil

Freshly grated
    parmesan

For the Pici pasta

For the ingredients of the Pici pasta dough see recipe on page 133. Take the room temperature pasta and cut into small pieces.

On a floured work surface, pinch the pasta through your fingers to make the rough shape of a skinny noodle. Roll out the noodle into a long, thin shape using your fingers, working from the center outward. Allow the pasta to dry for 30 to 40 minutes, then cook immediately in salted boiling water.

Method

Cook the pici pasta in a generous amount of salted boiling water. Drain the pasta and reserve warm.

Toss the cooked pasta with salt and a generous amont of black pepper, olive oil and parmesan. Serve warm with a sprinkle of parmesan and olive oil.

Coniglio alla contadina

PEASANT STYLE
BRAISED RABBIT

Ingredients

One 3 pound rabbit

1 small red onion,
    peeled & chopped

1 pound roma or plum
    tomatoes, peeled
    and chopped

2 garlic cloves, peeled
    and chopped

4 fresh rosemary sprigs

3 cups dry white wine

Vegetable stock
    (see page 133 for
    recipe)

Olive oil

Salt and pepper

Method

Clean and quarter the rabbit. In a large heavy-bottomed sauce pan, heat 4 table-spoons of olive oil and sauté the onion and garlic until golden brown. Season the rabbit quarters with salt and pepper on all sides. Add the seasoned rabbit to the pan and brown the rabbit on all sides.

Once the rabbit is browned, add the wine and bring the mixture to the boil. Turn down to a simmer and cover. Cook the rabbit, covered, for 15 minutes, them add the toma-toes and rosemary. Season with salt and pepper and continue to cook for another 20 minutes, gradually adding some vegetable stock as needed to maintain some moisture in the pan. Once the rabbit is fully cooked, pour the remaining juices over the top.

"He was so close, I could see the moisture glistening
on his lip, and still smell the kiss we'd just ended."

MEMOIRS OF A GEISHA by AURTHUR GOLDEN, 1997

Antipasti misti
MIXED COLD APPETIZER

Spaghetti alla salsiccia, olive nere, funghi e pomodori
SPAGHETTI WITH PORK SAUSAGE, KALAMATA OLIVES, MUSHROOMS AND TOMATOES

Fritto misto di pollo, coniglio e verdure
FRIED CHICKEN, RABBIT AND VEGETABLES

Antipasti misti
MIXED COLD APPETIZER

Spaghetti alla salsiccia, olive nere, funghi e pomodori
SPAGHETTI WITH PORK SAUSAGE, KALAMATA OLIVES, MUSHROOMS AND TOMATOES

Fritto misto di pollo, coniglio e verdure
FRIED CHICKEN, RABBIT AND VEGETABLES

Antipasti misti

MIXED COLD APPETIZER

"Arrange your favorite cold cuts of meat and olives and nuts on a serving plate. Garnish with edible flowers. You can also use roasted peppers, fresh mozzarella, toasted Tuscan bread and parmesan chunks of cheese if you wish."

Ingredients

Peppers stuffed with
    prosciutto and
    parmesan

Salami

Kalamata olives

1 lemon, zested

1 orange, zested

Olive oil

Chile flakes

Roasted Hazelnuts

Edible flowers like Johnnie
    jump ups and

Nasturtium

Spicy Kalamata Olives
Add the lemon and orange zest to the kalamata olives along with some olive oil and chile flakes, and heat in a pan until warm.

Spaghetti alla salsiccia, olive nere, funghi e pomodori

SPAGHETTI WITH PORK SAUSAGE, KALAMATA OLIVES, MUSHROOMS AND TOMATOES

Ingredients

12 ounces spaghetti

4 to 5 ounces pork
    sausage, rough
    chopped

20 pitted kalamata
    olives, chopped

2 to 3 porcini mushrooms,
    chopped

Roma or plum tomatoes,
    peeled and chopped

Olive oil

20 fresh Italian parsley
    leaves, chopped

Salt and black pepper

Method
Cook the spaghetti in a generous amount of boiling salted water. Drain the spaghetti and reserve warm.

Meanwhile in a heavy-bottomed sauté pan heat one tablespoon of olive oil and saute the sausage. Cook the sausage for four to five minutes or until fully cooked. Remove the sausage to drain on paper towels and discard the leftover oil. In the same pan heat one tablespoon of olive oil and saute the mushrooms and garlic. Add the kalamata olives and tomatoes and sauté for one to two minutes more.

Add the cooked sausage to the pan and continue cooking for seven to ten minutes or until the liquid is almost absorbed. Once the sauce is cooked down, season with salt and pepper and add the parsley. Toss the sauce with the warm cooked spaghetti and serve hot immediately.

Fritto misto di pollo, coniglio e verdure

MIXED FRIED CHICKEN, RABBIT AND VEGETABLES

Ingredients

2 chicken legs, boned and
    chopped into
    8 pieces
2 rabbit hind legs, boned
    and chopped into
    8 pieces
1 small zucchini
1 small carrot
1 small yellow squash
5 to 6 fresh squash blossoms
2 cups all-purpose flour
2 teaspoons cayenne
    pepper
Salt and pepper
3 to 4 cups peanut oil
for frying
1 lemon cut into wedges

Method

In a heavy-bottomed frying pot, heat the peanut oil to 350 degrees Fahrenheit. In a mixing bowl, combine the all-purpose flour and cayenne pepper. Season the flour with salt and pepper. Dredge the chicken and rabbit in the flour separately. Cut the zucchini, carrot and yellow squash into batons and dredge in the seasoned flour. Carefully slip the dredged chicken into the hot oil and fry until golden brown and fully cooked, about 4 to 5 minutes. Then carefully remove the chicken onto paper towels to drain. Repeat this process with the rabbit. Once the chicken and rabbit are fried, begin frying the vegetables one at a time and carefully remove onto paper towels to drain. Season each batch of rabbit, vegetables and chicken with salt and pepper as they are removed from oil. Serve hot with fresh lemon wedges.

"She still haunts me phantomwise,
Alice moving under skies.
Never seen by waking eyes."

THROUGH THE LOOKING GLASS by LEWIS CARROLL, 1877

STRADA MENU

Spaghetti con pomodori secchi e basilico
SPAGHETTI WITH SUNDRIED TOMATO AND BASIL

Scallopini di vitello al limone ed avocado
VEAL SCALLOPINI WITH LEMON AND AVOCADO

Pomodori ripieni all'arugula
RIPE TOMATOES STUFFED WITH FAVA BEANS AND ARUGULA

Spaghetti con pomodori secchi e basilico
SPAGHETTI WITH SUNDRIED TOMATO AND BASIL

Scallopini di vitello al limone ed avocado
VEAL SCALLOPINI WITH LEMON AND AVOCADO

Pomodori ripieni all'arugula
RIPE TOMATOES STUFFED WITH FAVA BEANS AND ARUGULA

Spaghetti con pomodori secchi e basilico

SPAGHETTI WITH
SUN DRIED TOMATO
AND BASIL

Ingredients

12 ounces spaghetti

6 to 8 ounces sun dried

tomatoes

20 leaves fresh basil

Olive oil

Salt and pepper

Freshly grated

parmesan cheese

Method

Roughly chop the sun dried tomatoes and soak them in warm water for 20 minutes.

Remove the tomatoes from the warm water and pat dry with absorbent paper towels. Roughly chop the fresh basil leaves.

Cook the spaghetti in a generous amount of boiling salted water. Drain the pasta and toss with the tomatoes and basil. Add a generous splash of olive oil and season with salt and pepper. Garnish with parmesan cheese, fresh cracked black pepper and more basil leaves.

Scallopini di vitello al limone ed avocado

VEAL SCALLOPINI
WITH LEMON
AND AVOCADO

Ingredients

1 pound trimmed

veal loin

1/4 cup all-purpose

flour

2 tablespoons unsalted

butter

Juice of one lemon

1 peeled garlic clove,

chopped

1 tablespoon capers

1 avocado

Edible flowers

(see page 135)

Salt and black pepper

20 leaves Italian

parsley, chopped

Method

Cut the veal loin into 4 portions and place portions between 2 pieces of waxed paper or plastic wrap. Pound the veal portions to 1/8-inch thick.

Season the pounded veal with salt and pepper on both sides and dust with the flour. In a heavy-bottomed sauté pan, add half of the butter and sauté the veal until golden brown on both sides.

Remove the veal portions from the pan and add the remaining butter. Heat the butter until it is golden brown then add the garlic and sauté .

Add the capers, lemon juice and parsley and season with salt and pepper to taste. Allow the sauce to thicken slightly, then pour over the sautéed veal portions. Garnish with avocado slices and edible flowers. Serve immediately.

Pomodori ripieni all'arugula d'estate e fave

RIPE TOMATOES STUFFED WITH SUMMER ARUGULA AND FAVA BEANS

"Fava beans are found all over Tuscany and I love their versatility and beautiful green shell. When the sun is hot in the middle of summer the arugula is very spicy and that's when this dish is best!"

Ingredients for the fava beans

1/2 cup fresh fava beans, peeled
2 cloves peeled garlic
Salt

Ingredients for the sauce

2 small green onions, thinly sliced
1 small garlic clove, peeled thinly sliced
5 sprigs Italian parsley, leaves only, chopped
Extra-virgin olive oil
Red wine vinegar
Salt and black pepper

Garnish

2 large ripe tomatoes
Fresh arugula leaves
Extra-virgin olive oil

Prepare the Fava beans

Add the fava beans and garlic to a stock pot with a generous amount of boiling water. Let the beans simmer for approximately 2 minutes or until tender. You want the beans to be soft but still retain their shape.

Drain the beans. Place them in a bowl to cool and cover with ice water.

Prepare the sauce

Add the green onions, garlic and parsley to a mixing bowl and season to taste with extra-virgin olive oil, red wine vinegar, salt and pepper. Mix well and refrigerate for 1 hour.

Prepare the tomatoes

Cut off the top part of the tomato then scoop out the pulp and seeds from the bottom part. Season the inside of the tomato with salt and black pepper.

To assemble

Line the inside part of the tomatoes with the arugula leaves, allowing the leaves to stick out of the tomatoes. Add the basil leaves to the beans, mix again and stuff the tomatoes.

Pour a few extra drops of extra-virgin olive oil over the top and serve immediately.

"At his lips' touch she blossomed for him like a flower
and the incarnation was complete."

THE GREAT GATSBY by F. SCOTT FITZGERALD, 1929

Risotto alle cipolle ed aceto balsamico
RICE WITH CARAMELIZED ONIONS AND BALSAMIC VINEGAR

Ossobuco
BRAISED VEAL SHANKS

Piselli al prosciutto
PEAS WITH PROSCIUTTO

Risotto alle cipolle ed aceto balsamico
RICE WITH CARAMELIZED ONIONS AND BALSAMIC VINEGAR

Ossobuco
BRAISED VEAL SHANKS

Piselli al Prosciutto
PEAS WITH PROSCIUTTO

Risotto alle cipolle ed aceto balsamico

RICE WITH CARAMELIZED ONION AND BALSAMIC VINEGAR

Ingredients

2 cups homemade
    chicken stock (see
    page 133 for recipe)
5 tablespoons
    unsalted butter
2 small white onions,
    peeled & chopped
1 cup arborio rice
1/2 cup dry white wine
1/2 cup freshly grated
    parmesan cheese
1 to 2 tablespoons fresh
    chopped thyme
Salt and black pepper
1/2 cup balsamic vinegar

Method

Heat the chicken stock and reserve warm. In a heavy-bottomed saute pan heat two tablespoons of butter and sauté the onions.

Continue sautéeing the onions until they become caramelized and golden brown on all sides. Remove the onions from the pan and reserve at room temperature until needed. Add the rice to the hot pan and 1 tablespoon of butter. Coat each grain of rice with the butter and sauté until the rice starts to become golden brown. Add the white wine and cook until the wine is absorbed. Add enough warm chicken stock to just cover the rice and stir while liquid is being absorbed.

Continue cooking and stirring with small additions of stock as previous addition of stock is absorbed. This takes approximatley 12 to 15 minutes. Season with salt and pepper to taste.When the rice is cooked, add the caramelized onions and 1/2 cup of balsamic vinegar and continue to cook until the balsamic is absorbed. Stir in 1 to 2 tablepoons of butter and the parmesan cheese to the rice.

Ossobuco

BRAISED VEAL SHANKS

Ingredients

For the ossobuco:
Four 2 inch crosscuts
    of veal hind shanks
1/2 cup all
    purpose flour
1/4 cup unsalted butter
1 tablespoon olive oil
1 small white onion,
    peeled & chopped
2 celery stalks,
    chopped
1 small carrot, peeled
    and chopped
2 peeled garlic cloves,
    chopped
4 roma tomatoes,
    chopped
12 to 16 ounces Chianti
    Classico
Salt and black pepper

Method

Pre heat the oven to 300 degrees Fahrenheit.

Dust each piece of veal shank with flour, salt and pepper. In a large heavy bottomed casserole, heat half the butter and all the oil.

Brown all sides of the seasoned and dusted veal shanks. Remove the browned veal shanks from the pan and let rest at room temperature.

Discard the oil and butter from the pan. Add the remaining butter to the pan and sauté the onion, carrot, garlic until golden brown. Add the celery and sauté for 2 minutes more. Add the wine to the sautéed vegetables and bring to a boil. Once the red wine is boiling, add the browned veal shanks and tomatoes. Bring back to the boil and cover. Place the casserole in the preheated oven and cook for 2 1/2 hours, or until the veal is tender and almost falling off the bone. Remove the ossobuco from the wine and vegetables and reserve warm.

Reduce the wine and vegetables over medium high heat to desired consistency. Spoon some of the thickened sauce around the shanks and serve immediately.

Piselli al prosciutto
PEAS WITH PROSCIUTTO

Ingredients
1/2 cup homemade
 chicken stock
 (page 132 for recipe)
10 ounces fresh or
 frozen green peas
1 tablespoon olive oil
1 shallot thinly sliced
2 ounces chopped
 prosciutto
 or cooked
 bacon
Salt and pepper

Method
Using a heavy-bottomed saucepan, heat the chicken stock and add the peas. Cook for 4 to 5 minutes or until tender. Drain and reserve peas. In a heavy-bottomed sauté pan heat the olive oil and sauté the shallot until tender. Add the prosciutto and peas and sauté for 2 to 3 minutes. Season with salt and pepper and serve immediately.

"The girl smiled with contentment when she opened her eyes and saw him,
and then, stretching her long legs languorously beneath the rustling sheets,
beckoned him into bed beside her, . . . "

CATCH 22 by JOSEPH HELLER, 1961

Crostini alla lepre
TOASTS WITH RABBIT RAGU

Gnocchi con salvia e burro
POTATO DUMPLINGS WITH SAGE AND CARAMELIZED BUTTER

Shinco di maiale arrosto
ROASTED PORK SHANK

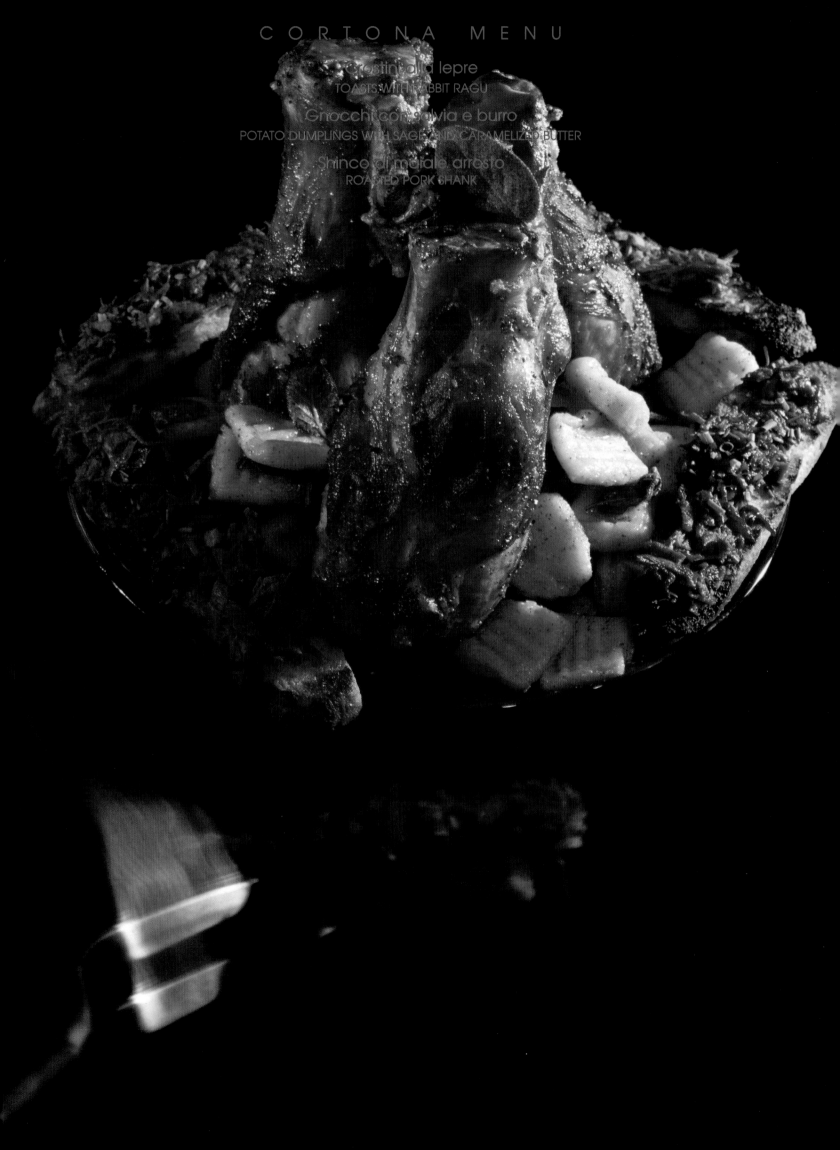

Crostini alla lepre
TOASTS WITH RABBIT RAGU

Gnocchi con salvia e burro
POTATO DUMPLINGS WITH SAGE AND CARAMELIZED BUTTER

Stinco di maiale arrosto
ROASTED PORK SHANK

Crostini alla lepre

TOASTS WITH
RABBIT RAGU

Ingredients

1 pound piece of
   hare or rabbit

1 tablespoon olive oil

1 ounce prosciutto,
   chopped

1 small white onion,
   chopped

1 celery stalk, chopped

1 small carrot, peeled
   and chopped

1 garlic clove, peeled
   and chopped

2 teaspoons all
   purpose flour

Pinch of freshly
   grated nutmeg

1 whole clove

Salt and black pepper

1 cup dry red wine

1/4 cup homemade
   veal stock (page 133
   for recipe)

4 slices toasted Tuscan
   bread (recipe, page 68)

Method

Cut the hare into medium size pieces. Warm the olive oil in a heavy-bottomed pan and sauté the onion and prosciutto for 5 minutes.

Add the celery, carrot, and hare pieces and sauté until the rabbit is golden brown, about 5 minutes. Season with flour, clove, nutmeg, salt and pepper. Pour in about 1/3 of the wine and veal stock and cook covered on low heat for 1 to 1 1/2 hours gradually adding the wine and stock as needed. Bone the hare and chop the meat coarsely. Return the meat to the pan and reserve warm. Top the toasted slices of Tuscan bread with the warm hare meat and serve warm.

Gnocchi con salvia e burro

POTATO DUMPLINGS
WITH SAGE AND
CARAMELIZED
BUTTER

Ingredients

2 1/2 pounds russet
   or baking potatoes

1-3/4 cups all-purpose flour

2 large egg yolks

1 large fresh bunch
   sage leaves

2 tablespoons
   unsalted butter

Salt and black pepper

Method

Bake the potatoes in their skins until tender. Peel the potatoes, place in a bowl and mash while still hot. Add half of the flour and egg yolks and season with salt and pepper. Quickly work the flour mixture into the potatoes to form a smooth dough. Flour a work surface and the palms of your hands and roll the dough into cylinders about 3/4 inch in diameter. Cut the cylinders into pieces about 1 inch long and roll a fork over them to make indentions on the surface. As the gnocchi are made place them on another lightly floured surface. Cook the gnocchi in a generous amount of boiling salted water, adding them a few at a time and removing them with a slotted spoon when they float. As the gnocchi are finished cooking in the water reserve warm on a plate. Heat the butter in a heavy-bottomed sauté pan until golden brown. Add the boiled gnocchi to the pan and season with salt and pepper. Add the sage and sauté for 2 to 3 minutes or until the butter is amber and the sage and gnocchi are golden brown and hot throughout.

Stinco di maiale arrosto

ROASTED PORK SHANKS

Ingredients

2 large pork shanks

6 fresh rosemary sprigs

6 fresh sage sprigs

Olive oil

Salt and black pepper

1 small white onion,
      peeled & quartered

2 garlic cloves,
      whole

1 small carrot,
      peeled and chopped

1 quart homemade
      veal stock (page 133
      for recipe)

1 cup dry red wine

Method

Preheat your oven to 300 degrees fahrenheit. In a heavy-bottomed braising dish warm 2 tablespoons of olive oil. Season the pork shanks with salt and pepper and sear in the braising dish until golden brown and caramelized on all sides.

Remove the browned pork shanks and rest at room temperature.

Add to the braising pan the onion, garlic and carrot and sauté for 5 minutes, stirring once or twice. Add the stock, wine, sage and rosemary to the sautéed vegetables and bring to a boil.

Add the browned pork shanks to the boiling liquid and immediately cover, with a lid or foil, and place in the preheated oven.

Cook covered for 1 1/2 hours or until tender and almost falling off the bone. Remove the tender pork shanks from the liquid and reduce the liquid on the stove top to desired sauce consistency. Spoon the reduced sauce over the warm pork shanks and serve immediately.

"Let his left hand be under my head and the right hand embrace me . . ."

SONG OF SONGS, 2:6-7

Pasta ai carciofi
ARTICHOKE PASTA

Polpettone
VEAL MEATLOAF

Verdure d'inverno arrosto
WINTER ROOT VEGETABLES ROASTED IN OLIVE OIL

Pasta ai carciofi
ARTICHOKE PASTA

Polpettone
VEAL MEATLOAF

Verdure d'inverno arrosto
WINTER ROOT VEGETABLES ROASTED IN OLIVE OIL

Pasta ai carciofi

ARTICHOKE PASTA

Ingredients

12 ounces spaghetti

2 large globe artichokes

1 tablespoon red
   chile flakes

2 cloves peeled garlic,
   chopped

2 ounces olive oil

Salt and black pepper

Method

Boil the artichokes whole in a generous amount of salted boiling water that has 1/3 of the chile flakes added. Cook the artichokes for 30 minutes or until tender. Save the water for cooking the pasta. Remove the outside leaves of the artichokes and save for garnish.

Clean the artichoke

(see page 92 for artichoke preparation) and slice the cooked heart and stem. In a heavy-bottomed sauté pan, heat the olive oil and add the garlic. Cook the garlic until golden brown then add the artichoke and remaining chile flakes and sauté for 2 or 3 minutes. Meanwhile cook the spaghetti in the left over boiling artichoke water, drain the pasta and toss with the sautéed artichokes. Garnish with the artichoke leaves and serve immediately.

Polpettone

VEAL MEATLOAF

Ingredients

4 ounces pancetta
   or bacon

2 cloves peeled garlic

1 tablespoon chopped
   rosemary leaves

2 pounds ground
   veal shoulder

3 large eggs

4 tablespoons freshly
   grated parmesan

Salt and pepper

Method

Preheat your oven to 375 degrees Fahrenheit. Using a

meat grinder, coarsely grind the pancetta, garlic and rosemary. Add the ground veal shoulder and the ground pancetta mixture to a mixing bowl and stir together. Add the parmesan and eggs and season with salt and pepper. Mix the ingredients well. Place the veal mixture on a prepared baking tray in an 8 inch long loaf and bake in the preheated oven for 50 minutes or until golden brown and cooked through. Serve immediately.

Verdure d'inverno arrosto

WINTER ROOT VEGETABLES
ROASTED IN OLIVE OIL

Ingredients

1 small celery root,
   peeled and diced

1 small rutabaga,
   peeled and diced

1 small purple top
   turnip, peeled
   and diced

2 fresh peeled garlic
   cloves, chopped

Olive oil

Salt and pepper

1 tablespoon fresh
   rosemary leaves,
   rough chopped

1 tablespoon fresh
   sage leaves, rough
   chopped

Method

Preheat your oven to 375 degrees Fahrenheit. In a heavy bottomed roasting pan, heat 1 to 2 tablespoons of olive oil.

Add the celery root, rutabaga, turnip, and garlic to the pan and sauté for 3 to 4 minutes over medium heat. Stir the vegetables occasionally and season with salt, pepper, rosemary and sage.

Once the vegetables start to color, place in the oven, uncovered for 20 to 30 minutes, or until tender and golden brown.

Stir the vegetables while roasting 2 to 3 times. Remove from the oven and serve warm.

"Perhaps when a man has held a woman in his arms,
there is a little of her with him forever."

THE WALKING DRUM by LOUIS L'AMOUR, 1985

Maccheroni all'affumicata
MACARONI WITH SMOKED MOZZARELLA

Pappa al pomodoro
TOMATO BREAD SOUP

Arista di maiale
ROASTED PORK LOIN WITH ROSEMARY

Maccheroni all'affumicata
MACARONI WITH SMOKED MOZZARELLA

Pappa al pomodoro
TOMATO BREAD SOUP

Arista di maiale
ROASTED PORK LOIN WITH ROSEMARY

Maccheroni all' affumicata

MACARONI WITH SMOKED MOZZARELLA

Ingredients

3 ounces smoked ham, chopped

4 ounces smoked mozzarella

1 tablespoon unsalted butter, plus extra for greasing baking dish

4 fresh sage leaves, chopped

1/2 cup heavy cream

2 tablespoon freshly grated parmesan cheese

Salt and pepper

1/2 pound macaroni

1 to 2 tablespoons dried, seasoned bread crumbs

Method

Preheat your oven to 375 degrees Fahrenheit. In a heavy-bottomed sauté pan, heat the butter and sauté the ham and sage for 3 to 4 minutes.

Add the cream, mozzarella and one tablespoon of parmesan to the ham and sage and gently heat the mixture until the cheese has melted. Season with salt and pepper. Remove the pan from heat and rest at room temperature. Cook the macaroni in a generous amount of salted boiling water. Drain the pasta and stir into the cheese sauce. Add the pasta and cheese sauce to a shallow greased baking dish and dust the top with the remaining parmesan cheese mixed with the bread crumbs. Cook in the preheated oven for 15 minutes or until the top is golden brown. Serve immediately.

Pappa al pomodoro

TOMATO BREAD SOUP

"A great summertime soup to make when the tomatoes and basil are at their best. Be sure to use a crusty, stale bread."

Ingredients for the soup

2 garlic cloves, peeled and cut into slivers

1/4 cup olive oil

2 pounds ripe summer tomatoes, peeled and seeded

8 slices stale Tuscan bread (page 68 for recipe)

1 large bunch fresh basil

Salt and black pepper

Olive oil, for serving

Prepare the soup

Put the garlic and olive oil in a heavy-bottomed saucepan and cook gently for 2 to 3 minutes. Let the garlic turn golden brown, then add the tomatoes. Simmer for 20 minutes, stirring occasionally, until the tomatoes become concentrated.

Season with salt and pepper, then add 2-1/2 cups water and bring to a boil. Cut most of the crust off the bread and break or cut into large chunks. Put the bread into the tomato mixture and stir gently until the bread absorbs the liquid, adding more boiling water if it is too thick. Remove from the heat and allow to cool slightly. Tear the basil leaves into pieces and stir into the soup with 1/4 to 1/2 cup of olive oil. Let sit before serving to allow the bread to absorb the flavor of the basil and oil. Serve in warm bowls and add a splash more of the olive oil.

Arrosto di maiale

ROASTED PORK LOIN WITH
ROSEMARY

Ingredients

One-12 ounce center
 cut pork loin roast
4 fresh sprigs rosemary,
 leaves only
3 peeled garlic cloves,
 sliced
Olive oil
Salt and pepper

Method

Preheat your oven to 325 degrees Fahrenheit.

Season the pork loin roast with salt and pepper on all sides. Using your sharpening steel or paring knife, make several insertions into the center and ends of the roast. Stuff the holes with the rosemary leaves and sliced garlic.

Place the pork loin on a baking sheet and splash a little olive oil over the top. Roast in the preheated oven for 1 hour or to desired doneness. Remove from the oven and let rest at room temperature for 5 minutes. Slice and serve immediately.

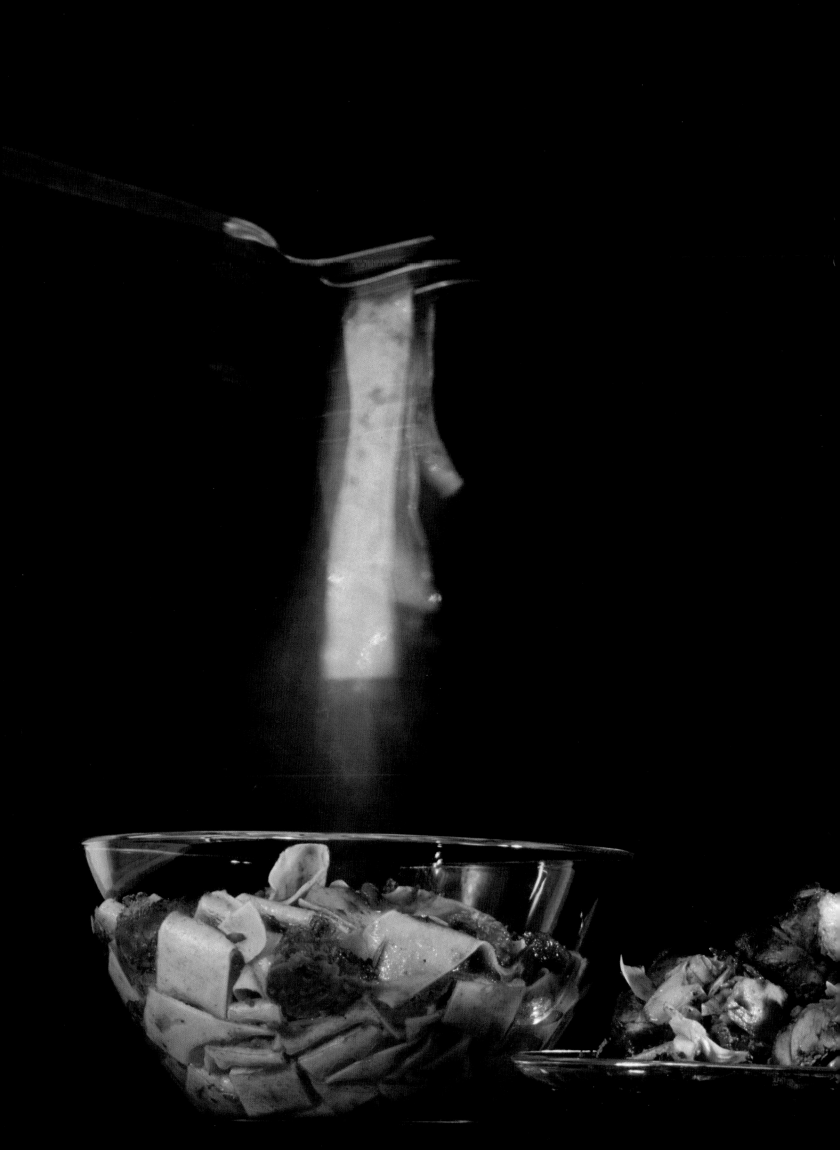

FIRENZE MENU

Pasta con cinghiale
EGG NOODLES WITH WILD BOAR

Tortellini con piselli ai funghi
TORTELLINI WITH PEAS AND MUSHROOMS

Stinco di agnello ripieno con carciofi
ARTICHOKE STUFFED LAMB SHANK

Broccoli di rape con peperoncini, aglio e olio
BROCCOLI RABE WITH CHILE, GARLIC AND OLIVE OIL

Pasta con cinghiale
EGG NOODLES WITH WILD BOAR

Tortellini con piselli ai funghi
TORTELLINI WITH PEAS AND MUSHROOMS

Stinco d'agnello ripieno con carciofi
ARTICHOKE STUFFED LAMB SHANK

Broccoli di rape con peperoncini, aglio ed olio
BROCCOLI RABE WITH CHILE, GARLIC AND OLIVE OIL

Pappardelle con cinghiale

PAPPARDELLE
WITH
WILD BOAR SAUCE

Ingredients

1 pound pappardelle
pasta (see semolina
pasta page)

1 pound wild boar
meat, from the leg

1 1/2 cups Chianti wine

1 small white onion,
chopped

Salt and black pepper

2 bay leaves

3 fresh rosemary sprigs

3 tablespoons olive oil

1 tablespoon
all-purpose flour

10 to 12 ounces roma
tomatoes, peeled
and chopped

Method
Cut meat into 1-1/2 inch cubes and place them in a bowl. Add the wine, onion, juniper berries, bay leaves and rosemary. Refrigerate and marinate for 12 hours. Drain off, strain and reserve the marinade. Dry the meat with paper towels.

In a heavy-bottomed shallow saucepan, warm the olive oil and add the meat.

Brown on all sides. Once the meat is browned, sprinkle in the flour and stir well. Add tomatoes and marinade and stir well. Bring the pan to a boil, then reduce the heat to a simmer. Cook covered, gently simmering for two hours, stirring occasionally. Season with salt and pepper and reserve warm.

For the Pappardelle
Roll the pasta through the pasta machine to setting one. Once the pasta is rolled into thin sheets, cut the pasta using a wheel cutter into long strips about 1 inch wide and 10 to `12 inches long. Allow the pasta to dry for 30 to 40 minutes. Cook the pappardelle (pasta) in a generous amount of boiling salted water. Drain the pasta and toss with the warm wild boar sauce. Serve immediately.

Tortellini con piselli ai funghi

TORTELLINI WITH PEAS
AND MUSHROOMS

Ingredients

1 recipe semolina pasta
(page 133 for recipe)

3 ounces ricotta

3 ounces freshly grated
parmesan, plus more
for garnish

1 tablespoon fresh
rosemary, chopped

2 ounces heavy cream

Olive oil

8 ounces fresh
green peas

6 ounces fresh porcini or

portobello mushrooms

Salt and black pepper

Method

Roll the pasta dough into a thin sheet. Using a round cutter, cut out discs. In a mixing bowl, mix together the ricotta, parmesan and rosemary. Season with salt, pepper and olive oil. Stuff the round discs with the cheese mixture and fold the discs in half. Pinch to seal. Wrap the "half moon" shaped pasta around your finger and pinch to seal. Complete the rest of the tortellini in the same manner. In a heavy-bottomed sauté pan, heat 1 tablespoon of olive oil and sauté the mushrooms and peas until tender. Add the cream and a pinch of parmesan to the peas and mushrooms and season with salt and pepper. Cook over medium heat until the sauce thickens. Meanwhile cook the Tortellini in a generous amount of boiling salted water. Drain the pasta and toss with the warm pea and mushroom mixture. Garnish with more grated parmesan and serve immediately.

(continues on page 48)

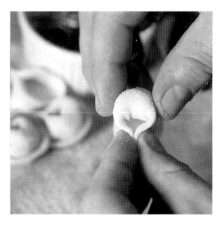

"She was entering upon marvels
where all would be passion, ecstasy, delirium."

MADAME BOVARY by GUSTAV FLAUBERT, 1857

Stinco d'agnello ripieno con carciofi

ARTICHOKE STUFFED
LAMB SHANKS

Ingredients

2 medium size fresh
    lamb shanks
2 large globe
    artichokes (page 92)
1 garlic clove, chopped
2 sprigs fresh rosemary
1 lemon, halved
Olive oil
Salt and black pepper

Method

Remove the bones from the lamb shanks. Pound to 1/4" thick. Season the lamb with salt, pepper and olive oil. Rub the garlic into the inside of the lamb where the bone was removed. Lay the rosemary on top of the garlic rubbed lamb and refrigerate covered for 1 to 2 hours. Meanwhile cook the artichokes in a generous amount of salted boiling

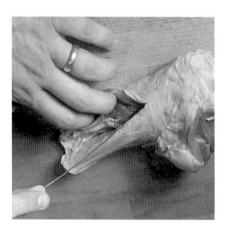

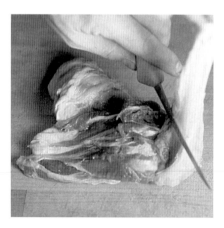

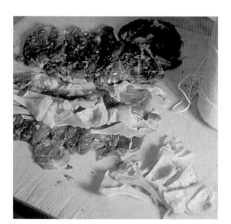

water. Add the lemon to the water while the artichokes are cooking. Cook the artichokes until tender, then remove and discard all the leaves and the inner choke. Slice the cleaned artichoke hearts and divide on top of the lamb shanks. Close the lamb shanks concealing the artichokes and rosemary inside and tie up with butcher's twine. Preheat your oven to 350 degrees Fahrenheit.

In a heavy-bottomed roasting pan heat 1 tablespoon of olive oil and sauté the prepared lamb shanks on all sides until golden brown. Place the seared lamb shanks in the oven and roast for 20 to 30 minutes, turning occasionally, or until cooked to desired doneness. Remove the lamb shanks from the oven and let rest at room temperature for 3 to 5 minutes. Remove the butcher's twine. Slice

the cooked lamb shanks and divide onto 2 warm plates. Serve immediately.

Broccoli di rape con peperoncini, aglio ed olio

BROCCOLI RABE WITH GARLIC, CHILE AND OLIVE OIL

Ingredients

8 ounces fresh

broccoli rabe (tough stems removed)
1 garlic clove, chopped
1 teaspoon red chile flakes
Olive oil
Salt and black pepper

Method

In a generous amount of boiling salted water cook the broccoli rabe for one minute. Transfer the cooked broccoli to a large ice and water bath and cool for 3 to 4 minutes.

Transfer to paper towels to drain. In a large heavy-bottomed sauté pan heat 1 tablespoon of olive oil. Sauté the garlic until it starts to turn golden brown, then add the broccoli rabe, chile flakes, salt and pepper. Sauté for 3 to 4 minutes stirring constantly.

Serve warm.

"If I saw you everyday, forever, I'd remember this time."

Hannibal by Thomas Harris, 1999

LUCCA MENU

Crostini alla fiorentina
TOASTS WITH CHICKEN LIVER

Ribolitta
HEARTY WINTER VEGETABLE SOUP

Pollo alla "creta"
CHICKEN BAKED IN CRUST

Crostini alla Fiorentina
TOASTS WITH CHICKEN LIVER

Ribolitta
HEARTY WINTER VEGETABLE SOUP

Pollo alla "creta"
CHICKEN BAKED IN CRUST

Crostini alla Fiorentina

TOAST WITH CHICKEN LIVER

Ingredients

6 fresh chicken livers

1 ounce sweet white wine

1 ounce capers, drained

1 tablespoon olive oil

1 tablespoon unsalted
   butter

12 Italian parsley
   leaves, chopped

4 slices Tuscan bread,
   toasted and rubbed
   with raw garlic

Method

In a heavy-bottomed sauté pan, warm the oil and butter and sauté the chicken livers until well colored and cooked through, about 2 minutes. Add the wine and continue cooking until the wine is almost absorbed. Add the capers and parsley leaves and transfer the ingredients to a food processor. Puree the ingredients and season with salt and pepper. The consisten-cy should be that of a thick paste. Add more wine if it is too thick. Serve warm or at room temperature on toasted Tuscan bread. Sprinkle more parsley on top.

Ribolitta

HEARTY WINTER SOUP

Ingredients

1 cup dried cannellini
   beans

1 pound black cabbage
   or savoy cabbage

9 tablespoons olive oil

1 white onion, peeled
   and chopped

1 tablespoon tomato paste

3 roma or plum tomatoes,
   peeled and chopped

3 celery stalks, diced

3 small carrots, peeled
   and diced

8 cups water

1 tablespoon fresh thyme
   leaves

Salt and black pepper

2 to 3 parmigiano
   reggiano heels

6 slices Tuscan bread,
   toasted and rubbed
   with raw garlic

1 bunch kale, optional

Method

In a bowl, cover the beans with cold water and soak for 12 hours. Once the beans are soaked, drain them and set aside. Remove and discard the hard stalks from the cabbage leaves. Slice the cabbage leaves roughly and set aside. In a heavy bottomed saucepan, warm 3 tablespoons of the olive oil and sauté the onion until it becomes translucent, about 4 to 5 minutes. Add the tomato paste, carrot and celery and continue cooking, stirring frequently for 4 to 5 minutes. Add the cabbage and stir to incorporate. Add the water, beans, parmesan heels and thyme. Season with salt and pepper. Bring the soup to the boil and reduce to a simmer. Cover and cook for 2 hours. Once the soup has simmered covered for 2 hours, pour the soup into a large bowl atop the toasted Tuscan bread and allow to cool completely. To serve, reheat the soup and season with salt and pepper, if necessary, and place in warm bowls. Top with the remaining olive oil. This soup is even better on the second day.

Pollo alla "creta"
CHICKEN BAKED IN CRUST

Ingredients
One-2 1/2 to 3 pound
free range chicken

3 sprigs fresh rosemary

3 sprigs fresh sage

6 oz. sweet Italian sausage

6 to 8 slices prosciutto

Salt and black pepper

For the crust

3 cups all-purpose flour

1 1/2 cups salt

1 cup plus 2 tablespoons
cold water

Method
Preheat your oven to 375 degrees Fahrenheit. Wash and dry the chicken very well. Stuff the rosemary, sage and sausage in the cavity of the bird. Place the prosciutto slices all over the breast of the bird. Season the inside and outside of the chicken lightly with salt and pepper and set aside while you prepare the crust. For the crust, place the flour in a mound on a board and make a well in the center. Place the salt in the well of the flour and add the water to the center of the well. Using a fork, slowly incorporate the flour into the water

and salt until a dough forms. Roll out the dough into a circular shape large enough to wrap around the bird. Wrap the bird with a large piece of parchment paper, making sure the bird is securely enclosed and that there are no holes in the parchment paper. Place the parchment-wrapped bird on the dough and wrap the dough around the bird. Transfer the bird to a baking sheet and place in the preheated oven. Bake the chicken for 1 hour. Once the bird is finished cooking, remove from the oven and cut the top off of the crust. Remove the bird from the crust and remove the parchment paper. Discard the crust and parchment paper and serve hot.

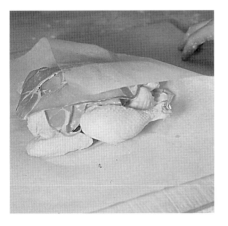

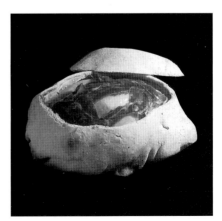

"My passions, concentrated on a single point resemble the rays of a sun assembled by a magnifying glass; they immediately set fire to whatever object they find in their way."

JUSTINE by MARQUIS DE SADE, 1780

Spaghetti alla carbonara
SPAGHETTI WITH EGG AND BACON

Pollo alla diavola
DEVIL STYLE CHICKEN

Carote dorate al burro con salvia
BUTTERED CARROTS WITH SAGE

Spaghetti alla carbonara
SPAGHETTI WITH EGG AND BACON

Polleto alla diavola
DEVIL STYLE CHICKEN

Carote dorate al burro con salvia
BUTTERED CARROTS WITH SAGE

Carote dorate al burro e salvia

BUTTERED CARROTS WITH SAGE

Ingredients

1/2 pound baby carrots
   peeled
2 quarts water
1 tablespoon salt
2 tablespoons butter
1 tablespoon chopped
   fresh sage leaves

Method

In a heavy-bottomed sauce pan, boil the water and salt. Add the carrots and boil 2 to 3 minutes or until tender. Remove the carrots from the water and place in an ice and water bath. Once the carrots are cooled, remove and dry with absorbent paper towels. In a heavy-bottomed sauté pan, heat the butter and sauté the carrots until golden brown, about 2 to 3 minutes. Season with salt and pepper, add the sage leaves and sauté for 1 minute more. Serve immediately.

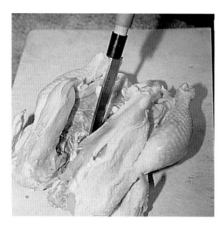

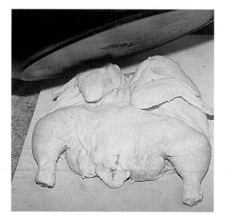

Polleto alla diavola

DEVIL STYLE CHICKEN

Ingredients

One-1 1/2 to 2 pound
   free range chicken
1 cup crushed red pepper
1 tablespoon salt
1/2 cup olive oil
5 to 6 fresh lemon wedges
1 or 2 fresh tulip flowers,
   petals for garnish
   (see page 135 for edible
   flowers)

Method

Cut the chicken along the length of the breast bone. First, using your hands, carefully flatten the chicken. Then, using a large iron skillet, flatten the chicken on a very solid surface. Do not worry about a few broken bones, this is the Italian way. This method is used so that the chicken is about one-inch thick. Grilling is quick and the chicken cooks evenly and maximizes the charcoal and spice flavors. Rub the red pepper into the skin and flesh of both sides of the chicken. Then repeat with salt and olive oil, being sure that each addition of seasonings is well absorbed. Cover and marinate for 2 hours refrigerated. Prepare your charcoal grill while the chicken is marinating. Be sure to build a large fire and let it burn down to glowing embers. Hard woods like hickory and oak work well. Once the fire is ready, place the chicken skin side down. Put an iron skillet on top of the grilling chicken and cook with the skillet on the top of the bird for at least 15 minutes, then turn. Baste with olive oil and lemon juice 3 or 4 times. The chicken is done when the outside is crisp and caramelized and the inside is firm but juicy. Serve the grilled chicken with a splash of lemon juice and olive oil over the top and fresh lemon wedges. Garnish with edible flowes.

Spaghetti alla carbonara

SPAGHETTI WITH EGG
AND BACON

Ingredients

4 ounces pancetta,

cut into match sticks

2 teaspoons olive oil

2 egg yolks

1 to 2 ounces

heavy cream

1 cup freshly grated

parmesan

12 ounces spaghetti

Salt and black pepper

Method

In a large heavy-bottomed sauté pan, heat the olive oil and sauté the pancetta slowly so that it releases its own fat before becoming crisp. Add some black pepper while the pancetta is cooking.

In a bowl, mix the egg yolks with the cream and season with salt and pepper. Add half of the parmesan to the mixture and whip until well mixed, about one minute.

Meanwhile cook the spaghetti in a generous amount of boiling salted water, then drain thoroughly. Add the cooked pasta to the hot pancetta in the sauté pan, and pour in the cream mixture.

Stir constantly so as to coat each piece of pasta, about 1 minute. Stir in the remanning parmesan, season with salt and pepper and serve on warm plates.

"She burns me, binds me, holds me,
seems like sugar to me."

UNFINISHED SONNET by MICHELANGELO, 1507

Calamari ripieni con salsiccia
SQUID STUFFED WITH SAUSAGE

Fagiano con prosciutto
PHEASANT WRAPPED IN PROSCIUTTO

Cippolini nell'aceto balsamico
CIPPOLINI ONIONS IN BALSAMIC VINEGAR

Calamari ripieni con salsiccia
SQUID STUFFED WITH SAUSAGE

Fagiano con prosciutto
PHEASANT WRAPPED IN PROSCIUTTO

Cippolini nell'aceto balsamico
CIPPOLINI ONIONS IN BALSAMIC VINEGAR

Calamari ripieni con salsiccia

SQUID STUFFED WITH SAUSAGE

Ingredients

4 medium squid, no
   bigger than your hand
4 oz. fresh Italian sausage
   (removed from casings)
8 roma or plum tomatoes,
   peeled
2 garlic cloves
2 sprigs fresh rosemary,
   leaves only
2 sprigs fresh sage,
   leaves only
1/2 cup dry red wine
1 small white onion,
   chopped
Salt and black pepper

Method

Preheat your oven to 300 degrees Fahrenheit.

Clean the squid by removing the tentacles from the body and scrape out the innards of the body. Peel any dark skin from the body and rinse well. Stuff the sausage into the whole bodies of the cleaned squid. Seal the end of the squid with a toothpick and refrigerate until needed.

In a blender, combine and puree the tomatoes, garlic, rosemary, sage, red wine and onion. Season the tomato mixture with salt and pepper. Add the tomato mixture to a heavy-bottomed braising pan and heat the mixture to the boil. Carefully add the stuffed squid to the hot tomato mixture and turn the heat down so it is just simmering. Cover the pan and place in the preheated oven. Cook the squid covered for 25 to 30 minutes. Add the cleaned tentacles to the tomato braising liquid for the last 6 to 8 minutes of cooking. Carefully remove the squid from the hot liquid, remove the toothpicks, slice and serve immediately.

Fagiano con prosciutto

PHEASANT WRAPPED
IN PROSCIUTTO

Ingredients

2 small pheasants
6 fresh thyme sprigs
6 slices prosciutto
2 fresh porcini or portabello
   mushrooms, sliced
15 leaves Italian
   parsley, chopped
Olive oil
2 garlic cloves, peeled
   and chopped
1-1/4 cups dry red wine
1 tablespoon
   unslated butter

Method

Preheat your oven to 450 degrees Fahrenheit.

Season the pheasants inside and out, and put the thyme sprigs in the cavities. Place the prosciutto slices over the breast and legs of the birds and tie them on with butcher's string.

In a small sauté pan, heat 2 tablespoons of olive oil and sauté the mushrooms. Then season with salt and pepper and add the garlic and parsley.

Continue sautéeing for 1 to 2 minutes, then set aside at room temperature until needed.

In a large roasting pan, heat 3 tablespoons of olive oil, and brown the birds on all sides. Once browned, add the birds to the hot oven and roast for 10 minutes. Turn the birds over. add the mushrooms and half the wine and continue cooking for another 5 to 10 minutes.

Remove the cooked birds and place on two warm plates. Deglaze the pan with the remaning wine and season with salt, pepper and butter.

Reduce the wine and mushrooms in the pan to a sauce consisitency and pour over the birds.

Serve immediately.

Cippolini nell' aceto balsamico

CIPPOLINI ONIONS IN BALSAMIC VINEGAR

Ingredients

12 fresh cippolini onions,
   peeled

2 cups balsamic vinegar

2 sprigs fresh rosemary

Salt and black pepper

Method

Combine all the ingredients in a heavy-bottomed sauce pan and bring to the boil. Season with salt and pepper. Remove from the heat and allow the onions to cool completely in the balsamic vinegar. Serve at room temperature.

"She tenderly kissed me, she fondly caressed,
and then I fell gently to sleep on her breast. . ."

FOR ANNIE By EDGAR ALLAN POE, 1849

Pizza Capricciosa
SUPREME PIZZA

Risotto ai funghi e parmigiano
RICE WITH WILD MUSHROOMS AND PARMESAN

Piccione alla salvia
ROASTED SQUAB WITH SAGE, BLACK PEPPER AND OLIVE OIL

Pizza capricciosa
"SUPREME" PIZZA

Risotto ai funghi e parmigiano
RICE WITH WILD MUSHROOMS AND PARMESAN

Piccione alla salvia
ROASTED SQUAB WITH SAGE, BLACK PEPPER AND OLIVE OIL

Pizza capricciosa

"SUPREME" PIZZA

Ingredients

12 slices prosciutto

1 cup kalamata olives, pitted and sliced

3 medium size fresh porcini or portobello mushrooms

1 large egg, or 4 quail eggs at room temperature

8 ounces fine semolina flour

1-1/2 cups all-purpose flour

1 ounce fresh yeast or 2 packages active dry yeast

1 cup warm water

1 teaspoon salt

Method

Preheat your oven to 400 degrees Fahrenheit. Place 4 unglazed terracotta tiles on the middle rack of the oven.

In an electric mixing bowl, combine the semolina and all-purpose flour. Add the salt and incorporate. In a separate mixing bowl, combine the yeast and warm water, mix well. Add the yeast and water to the flour mixture and mix until the dough starts to come together. Place the dough on a floured surface and knead until an elastic dough is formed. Allow the dough to rise in a warm spot in the kitchen until doubled in size. Punch the dough down, to release all the gasses, and roll into a very thin round shape. Place the disc of dough on a round cookie pan and top with 3 ounces of tomato sauce. Add the prosciutto, olives and sliced mushrooms to the top evenly distributing the ingredients. Slide the prepared pizza off of the cookie pan onto the hot terracotta tiles in the preheated oven. Bake the pizza for 5 to 7 minutes, then crack the egg into the middle and continue cooking until the crust is crisp and fully cooked. Carefully remove the pizza from the oven by sliding the round cookie sheet underneath. Slice and serve immediately.

Risotto ai funghi e parmigiano

RICE WITH WILD MUSHROOMS AND PARMESAN

Ingredients

2 cups homemade chicken stock (page 133 for recipe)

4 ounces fresh mushrooms, such as porcini, portabello, morel, chanterelle

1 ounce dry black trumpet and or chanterelle mushrooms, pulverized

Unsalted butter

1 small white onion, chopped

1 cup arborio rice

1/2 cup dry red wine

Freshly grated parmesan

1 tablespoon fresh chopped thyme

Salt and black pepper

Method

Heat the chicken stock with the dry wild mushrooms and reserve warm. In a heavy-bottomed sauté pan heat 1 tablespoon of butter and sauté the onion. Once the onion is translucent add arborio rice and stir so that every grain is coated. Sauté rice and onion for 1 to 2 minutes more. Once the rice begins to toast add the red wine and cook until the wine is absorbed. Add enough chicken stock just to cover rice and stir while the stock is being absorbed. Continue cooking and stiring with small addititons of chicken stock as the stock is absorbed. Season with salt and pepper as you go during the approximate 12 to 15 minutes of cooking time for complete absorbtion. In another heavy-bottomed sauté pan, heat one tablespoon of butter and sauté the fresh wild mushrooms with the shallots and herbs. Season with salt and pepper and reserve warm. Once the rice is cooked add the sautéed mushroom mixture, a little more stock, one tablespoon of butter and a generous pinch of parmesan. Season with salt, pep-per and fresh herbs. Serve warm with shavings of parmesan on top.

Piccione
alla salvia

ROASTED SQUAB WITH SAGE, BLACK PEPPER AND OLIVE OIL

Ingredients

Two-8 ounce fresh
squab
6 fresh sprigs sage
Salt and black pepper
Olive oil

Method

In a heavy-bottomed roasting pan, heat 3 tablespoon olive oil. Season the birds on all sides with salt and pepper and stuff the birds with the sage. Brown the birds on all sides in the hot oil and place them in the preheated oven. Roast the birds for 20 to 25 minutes, turning once or twice during that time. Remove the birds from the oven and drizzle more olive oil over the top. Season with black pepper and serve immediately.

S U M M E R

Pane alla Toscana

TUSCAN BREAD

"Light and crusty, pane alla toscana is the basic bread of all Tuscany. Its flavor is kept neutral in order to maintain its adaptability. With the slightest alteration it metamorphoses into a whole other magnificence. Drip some olive oil and salt over the top or add your favorite herbs to the dough."

Ingredients

For the sponge
3/4 cup plus 1 tablespoon
   all-purpose flour
1 ounce fresh yeast or
   2 packages active
   dry yeast
1/2 cup warm water
Pinch of salt

For the dough
5 cups all purpose flour
1 3/4 cup warm water

Method

To prepare the sponge place the 3/4 cup of flour and the pinch of salt in a small bowl and make a well in the center.

Dissolve the yeast in the water, stirring with a wooden spoon.

Pour the dissolved yeast into the well and mix very thoroughly with the wooden spoon, until the flour is incorporated. Sprinkle the additional 1 tablespoon of flour over the sponge.

Then cover the bowl with a cotton dish towel and let rest in a warm place until the sponge has doubled in size, about 1 hour.

(You will notice the disappearance of the tablespoon of flour or the formation of large cracks on the surface.)

Arrange the 5 cups of flour in a bowl or on a board, then make a well in the center.

Place the sponge in the well along with 1/2 cup of the warm water. With a wooden

spoon, carefully mix all the ingredients in the well.

Then add the remaining water and start mixing with your hands. Keep mixing until all but 1/2 cup of the flour is incorporated.

Then knead the dough with the palm of your hands, in a folding motion, until it is

homogeneous and smooth, about 15 minutes, incorporating the remaining flour to keep the dough from sticking.

Give the dough the shape you desire (a long or round loaf), then place it in a floured cotton dish towel.

Wrap the dough tightly in the dish towel and let it rest in a warm place, until doubled in size, about 1 hour. Line bottom shelf of oven with unglazed terra-cotta tiles.

Preheat the oven to 375 degrees for twice as long as normal in order to adequately heat the terracotta tiles.

Once the dough is ready, quickly unfold the wrapped dough onto the tiles. Bake the bread for about 55 minutes or until it sounds hollow when tapped.

Do not open the oven for 30 minutes after you have placed the dough inside it. Let the bread cool on a rack before serving.

Makes 1 loaf.

"You, you are a sunbeam, a drop of dew, a bird's song!"

Quasimodo to La Esmeradia
THE HUNCHBACK OF NOTRE-DAME by VICTOR HUGO, 1831

MONTECATINI MENU

Prosciutto di Parma e melone
PARMA PROSCIUTTO WITH MELON AND MINT

Fettuccine con gamberi, peperoncini e olio
SEMOLINA FETTUCCINE WITH SHRIMP, RED PEPPER FLAKES, AND OLIVE OIL

Grissini
BREAD STICKS

Prosciutto di Parma e melone
PARMA PROSCIUTTO WITH MELON AND MINT

Fettuccine con gamberi, peperoncini ed olio
SEMOLINA FETTUCCINE WITH SHRIMP, RED PEPPER FLAKES, AND OLIVE OIL

Grissini
BREAD STICKS

Prosciutto di Parma e melone

PARMA PROSCIUTTO WITH
MELON AND MINT

"This classic paring is wonderful when you want to spend more time with your love than preparing the food. Make sure to use ripe melon and leave the fat on the prosciutto when slicing."

Ingredients
1 ripe melon such as
   honeydew,
   cantaloupe or the
   American favorite
   watermelon
10 thin slices of Parma
   prosciutto
Mint sprigs

To assemble
Cut the melon in half and scoop out the seeds. Slice the melon into serving size pieces and arrange on two appetizer plates with the sliced Parma prosciutto placed on top of the melon Garnish with mint leaves.

Fettuccine con gamberi, peperoncini ed olio

FETTUCCINE WITH SHRIMP, RED
PEPPER FLAKES AND OLIVE OIL

Ingredients
12 ounces fettuccine

10 large shrimp, peeled
   and de-veined

2 teaspoons red pepper
   flakes

Olive oil

Salt and pepper

20 Italian parsley leaves,
   chopped

Method
Cook the fettuccine in a generous amount of salted boiling water. Drain and reserve warm.

Meanwhile season the shrimp on both sides with salt and pepper. Sauté the shrimp in a heavy-bottomed sauté pan with a tablespoon of olive oil until the shrimp are pink and just cooked. Toss the warm pasta with olive oil, red pepper flakes, salt and pepper and arrange on two warm plates.

Top the pasta with the shrimp and garnish with the chopped parsley.

Grissini

GARLIC
BREAD STICKS

Ingredients
2 ounces fresh yeast

1 1/2 ounces sugar

1/4 cup warm water

2 cups warm milk

2 ounces melted butter

1 ounce salt

1/2 cup roasted garlic
   purée

3 tablespoons molasses

3 lbs. all purpose flour

Method
In a large mixing bowl, combine the yeast, sugar, water, milk and molasses with a whisk.

Allow the mixture to bloom for 2 to 3 minutes. Add the the roast garlic purée and whisk in to incorporate.

Add the flour and salt to another large mixing bowl and whisk together to incorporate. Make a well in the center of the flour and salt mixture.

Pour the wet ingredients into the center of the well and using a fork slowly incorporate the flour until all the moisture is absorbed and a soft dough has formed.

Turn out the dough onto a floured work surface and continue kneading the dough for 4 to 5 minutes. Allow the dough to rest for 15 to 20 minutes.

Once the dough has rested, roll out on a floured surface to a thickness of 1/8 inch. Cut the bread sticks using a pasta wheel or run through your pasta machine using the fettuccine attachment. Dust the strips with flour and store in the refrigerator until ready to bake or freeze.

Preheat your oven to 325 degrees Fahrenheit. Lay out the strips of bread sticks onto a non-stick baking surface (silpat) or parchment paper and allow to rise in a warm spot, 20 to 30 minutes.

Spray the bread sticks with roast garlic oil or olive oil and season with salt. Bake in the preheated oven for 5 to 7 minutes or until golden brown.

"Calmly, with a shy smiling wordlessness, she led him on
as if deeper into a humid white warm great flower of which their
two bodies side by side on the sofa were some of the petals."

IN THE BEAUTY OF THE LILIES BY JOHN UPDIKE, 1996

Dadolata di polenta
FRIED POLENTA CUBES IN SPICY TOMATO SAUCE

Braciole di vitella ripiena con tartufi
ROASTED VEAL CHOP STUFFED WITH TRUFFLES

Asparagi e formaggi al forno
ASPARAGUS GRATINÉ

Dadolata di polenta
FRIED POLENTA CUBES IN SPICY TOMATO SAUCE

Braciole di vitella ripiena con tartufi
ROASTED VEAL CHOP STUFFED WITH TRUFFLES

Asparagi e formaggi al forno
ASPARAGUS GRATINE

Dadolata di polenta

FRIED POLENTA CUBES IN SPICY TOMATO SAUCE

Ingredients
For the polenta
2 quarts cold homemade
chicken stock
(see page 133
for recipe)
3/4 pound coarse
yellow corn meal
Salt and black pepper

For the sauce
1 small red onion, peeled
2 cloves garlic, peeled
1/3 cup extra virgin olive oil
1/4 cup red wine vinegar
1 1/2 cups tomato juice
4 anchovy filets, packed in
oil, drained
A large pinch of hot
red pepper flakes
Salt and black pepper

To fry the polenta
1 quart peanut or
vegetable oil

Garnish
20 sprigs flat leaf Italian
Parsley, chopped
3 cloves garlic, thinly sliced

To prepare the polenta
In a large heavy-bottomed pot, bring the broth to a boil, then season with salt and black pepper to taste. In a very slow but steady stream, add the cornmeal all the while stirring with a flat wooden spoon. Continue stirring and cooking over medium heat for 40 to 50 minutes until the polenta is smooth and well cooked. Spread the cooked polenta out on to a slightly oiled smooth surface, such as marble or a cookie sheet, to a thickness of 1 inch and let cool completely.

To prepare the sauce
Finely chop the onion and the garlic. Heat the oil in a heavy-bottomed sauce pot and sauté the onion and garlic until translucent. Add the anchovies and smash them with the back of a fork. Season to taste with salt, pepper and hot red pepper flakes. Add the vinegar and let it cook until the vinegar completely evaporates, then add the tomato juice and reduce the sauce by 1/3. Meanwhile cut the polenta into 1 inch cubes. Heat the peanut oil in a fryer to 375 degrees. Fry the polenta cubes until golden brown on all sides. Drain the polenta on a paper towel and be sure to season with salt as soon as they come out of the fryer. When all the polenta cubes are ready, place a little of the sauce on a warm plate, top with the warm fried polenta cubes. Add a little sauce to the top of the cubes and garnish with the chopped parsley and sliced raw garlic.

Braciole di vitella ripiena con tartufi

ROASTED VEAL CHOP STUFFED WITH TRUFFLES

Ingredients
Two-8 ounce trimmed
veal chops

1 small white truffle

Olive oil

4 fresh rosemary leaves

4 fresh sage leaves

Salt and black pepper

Method

Preheat your oven to 350 degrees Fahrenheit. Using a paring knife, make a small pocket in the veal chops by inserting the knife horizontally. Slice the truffle into 8 to 10 slices and stuff into the veal chops. Stuff in the rosemary and sage leaves as well. Season both sides of the chops with salt and pepper. In a heavy-bottomed sauté pan heat 1 tablespoon of olive oil. Add seasoned and stuffed veal chops to hot pan and sauté on both sides until golden brown. Place seared veal chops in oven and roast for 4 minutes on each side or to desired doneness. Remove from oven, let rest for 2 to 3 minutes. Serve warm after resting.

Asparagi e formaggi al forno
ASPARAGUS GRATINE

Ingredients

8 ounces fresh aspara-
gus, green or white,
bottoms removed

Freshly grated
parmesan cheese

Salt and black pepper

Olive oil

Method

Preheat your oven to broil. In a generous amount of salted boiling water, quickly cook the asparagus, one minute only!

Remove the asparagus from the boiling water immediately into a large ice and water bath. Let rest in the ice bath for 3 to 4 minutes, then drain on paper towels.

Season the cooled asparagus with salt, pepper and olive oil and place in a medium sized casserole dish. Top the seasoned asparagus with some parmesan cheese and place under the broiler for 2 to 3 minutes or until the cheese has melted and is golden brown. Serve immediately.

"She had wonderfully beautiful hair and I
would lie sometimes and watch her twisting it
up in the light that came in the open door
and it shone even in the night as water shines
sometimes just before it is really daylight."

A FAREWELL TO ARMS by ERNEST HEMINGWAY, 1929

Zuppa di carciofi con crostini ai pomodori secchi
ARTICHOKE SOUP WITH DRIED TOMATO TOASTS

Braciole alla Fiorentina
FLORENTINE STEAK

Verdura mista
MARINATED AND GRILLED VEGETABLES

Zuppa di carciofi con crostini ai pomodori secchi
ARTICHOKE SOUP WITH DRIED TOMATO TOASTS

Braciole alla Fiorentina
FLORENTINE STEAK

Verdura mista
MARINATED AND GRILLED VEGETABLES

Zuppa di carciofi con crostini ai pomodori secchi
ARTICHOKE SOUP WITH DRIED TOMATO TOASTS

Braciole alla Fiorentina
FLORENTINE STEAK

Verdura mista
MARINATED AND GRILLED VEGETABLES

Zuppa di carciofi con crostini ai pomodori secchi

ARTICHOKE SOUP WITH DRIED
TOMATO TOASTS

Ingredients for the soup

4 globe artichokes

(see page 92 for

preparation)

2 tablespoons olive oil

1 tablespoon butter

1 small white, onion

peeled & chopped

2 garlic cloves, peeled

and chopped

1 tablespoon hot red

chile flakes

1 sprig fresh thyme

3 cups homemade

chicken stock (page

133 for recipe)

Salt and black pepper

Extra virgin olive oil, or

white truffle oil for

garnish

Freshly grated parmigiano

reggiano

Ingredients for the tomato crostini

2 slices of Tuscan bread

(see page 68 for recipe)

1/4 cup dried

tomatoes, soaked in

hot water

3 large basil leaves,

chopped

Extra virgin olive oil

Salt and black pepper

Prepare the soup

Remove the tough outer leaves of the artichokes and cut off the top leaves. Pare the stems down to the paler tender part.

Slice the artichokes into eighths. Remove the inner choke, which will be prickly and undesirable. Heat the olive oil and the butter in a heavy-bottomed sauce pan and sauté the onions over medium heat until golden brown. Add the garlic and the prepared artichokes. Sauté together stirring with a wooden spoon for 5 to 10 minutes. Add the chile flakes and thyme.

Heat the stock and season to taste with salt and pepper. Add just enough stock to cover the artichokes. Simmer, covered, until they are tender, usually about 15 minutes. In a blender, purée the soup. Return to the sauce pan and add a little more stock to desired consistency. Season to taste with salt and pepper.

Prepare the crostini
Toast the Tuscan bread on both sides and rub with raw garlic.

Chop the dried tomatoes and place them in a bowl. Add the basil and season with salt, black pepper and a drizzle of extra virgin olive oil. Top each slice of the Tuscan bread with the dried tomato mixture.

Serve the soup in hot bowls and top with freshly grated parmesan, extra virgin olive oil and tomato crostini.

Braciole alla Fiorentina con verdura mista alla griglia

FLORENTINE STEAK WITH MARINATED GRILLED VEGETABLES

"In the trattorias all over Tuscany you will find Florentine steaks cooked over char grills in their court-yards and grill rooms. The steaks will be between 2 to 3 inches thick and should have the bone left in. Often the steak will feed at least 2 people."

Ingredients

1 to 1 1/2 pound rib
  or porterhouse steak,
  on the bone
1/2 ounce each fresh
  rosemary and
  sage leaves
1 small zucchini
1 small squash
1 red bell pepper
1 yellow bell pepper
6 large basil leaves
1/2 ounce fresh
  marjoram leaves
2-3 ounces extra-virgin
Olive oil
Salt and black pepper

Method

Start a fire in your char grill with your favorite hard wood (hickory). Let the fire burn down so that you have mainly coals. Lower your rack so it sits just over the glowing embers and grill the steak on both sides until charred but without over-cooking the inside (5 to 6 minutes on each side for medium rare). Remove the steak and let it rest on a plate away from heat. While the fire is still hot, grill the red and yellow peppers until their skin is charred and black. Remove the peppers from the grill and allow to cool before removing their skin, stems and seeds. Once the peppers are cleaned, cut them into eighths lengthwise. At the same time you are grilling the peppers you should also grill the zucchini and squash; one to two minutes on each side for the zucchini and squash will be sufficient. In a heavy-bottomed sauté pan, add the olive oil and heat over the burning embers until the oil begins to smoke. Once the oil smokes, add the rosemary and sage leaves. Remove the hot oil and herbs from the heat, slice the resting steak and pour the hot oil over the slices of steak. Season the sliced steak and divide onto two warm dinner plates. In a bowl, toss the peppers, zuc-chini, squash, marjoram and basil together. Season with salt, black pepper and extra-virgin olive oil and divide onto the two plates with the sliced steak.

"He led her out over the field where the flowers rose in pale
blue waves to her knees and she felt their soft petals against
her bare flesh and she lay down among them and felt them
all about her, accepting her and embracing her,
and a kind of drukenness possessed her."

THE FIELD OF BLUE CHILDREN by TENNESSEE WILLIAMS, 1939

Crostini con pomodoro e basilico
TOASTS WITH TOMATO AND BASIL

Zuppa di piselli d'estate con prosciutto e crema fresca
SUMMER PEA SOUP WITH PROSCIUTTO AND CREME FRAICHE

Agnello arrosto
ROASTED RACK OF BABY LAMB WITH ROSEMARY AND MINT LEAVES

Crostini con pomodoro e basilico
TOASTS WITH TOMATO AND BASIL

Zuppa di piselli d'estate con prosciutto e crema fresca
SUMMER PEA SOUP WITH PROSCIUTTO AND CRÈME FRAÎCHE

Agnello arrosto
ROASTED RACK OF BABY LAMB WITH ROSEMARY AND MINT LEAVES

Crostini con pomodoro e basilico

TOASTS WITH TOMATO AND BASIL

"I love to start a summer meal with this very simple appetizer. If you have a garden or are wanting to start one tomatoes and basil should be on the list!"

Ingredients
Olive oil

Salt and black pepper

1 clove garlic, minced

4 fresh, very ripe roma
   tomatoes, peeled
   and chopped

1 oz. fresh basil, chopped

4 slices Tuscan bread
   (recipe page 68)

Method
Place the tomatoes in a bowl. Moisten them with olive oil and season with salt and pepper to taste. Add the basil. Set aside. Now mix some of the remaining olive oil with the garlic and brush each slice of bread with this flavored oil.

Toast both sides until the edges of the bread begin to brown. Top each slice of the toasted bread with the tomato mixture and serve.

Zuppa di piselli d'estate con prosciutto e crema fresca

SUMMER PEA SOUP WITH PARMA HAM AND CRÈME FRAÎCHE

"In the early summer the fields of Tuscany yield such tender sweet green peas. You can celebrate that sweet and succulent flavor in this recipe."

Ingredients
1 tablespoon olive oil

1 tablespoon butter

1 small white onion,
   peeled & chopped

1 peeled garlic clove,
   thinly sliced

5 large basil leaves

1 pound fresh green
   peas, shelled

2 cups homemade
   chicken stock
   (page 133 for recipe)

Salt and black pepper

Freshly grated parmigiano
   reggiano cheese

Extra-virgin olive oil

Method
In a large heavy-bottomed sauce pan, melt oil and butter and sauté onions and garlic over low heat until soft and translucent, about 15 minutes. Add peas and the stock and cook covered for about 5 minutes or until the peas are tender. Put the mixture into a blender and add the basil. Purée the mixture then return to the pan and season with salt and pepper. Serve sprinkled with parmesan and extra-virgin olive oil.

Agnello arrosto

ROASTED RACK OF BABY LAMB WITH ROSEMARY AND MINT LEAVES

Ingredients

2-8 ounce racks baby
    lamb, trimmed and
    bones cleaned

2 long sprigs fresh
    rosemary

2 bunches fresh mint

Olive oil

Salt and black pepper

4 peeled garlic cloves

1 cup dry red wine,
    like Chianti

1 tablespoon butter

Fresh rosemary and mint
    leaves for chopping

Method

Place half of the rosemary and mint In a heavy-bottomed roasting pan. Set the garlic cloves on top of the herbs. Season the lamb with salt and pepper and wrap the exposed bones individually with tin foil. Set the two racks of lamb on top of the garlic and herbs. Top the racks of lamb with the remaining herbs and a splash of olive oil. Roast at 400 degrees Fahrenheit for 20 to 25 minutes, or to desired doneness. Remove the lamb and rest on a plate away from the heat. Discard any excess oil left in the roasting pan. Add the red wine to the roasting pan with the herbs and garlic and cook over medium heat until reduced to a sauce consistency. Stir the butter into the reduced wine and pour the sauce and herbs through a fine mesh strainer, making sure to press all of the sauce out of the herbs and garlic. Pour the strained sauce over the roasted lamb and serve with fresh chopped mint and rosemary.

"According to my belief, Dulcinea's eyes must be green emeralds,
full and large, with twin rainbows to serve as eyebrows."

DON QUIXOTE by CERVANTES, 1614

CARRARA MENU

Crostini all'olive nere
TOASTS WITH BLACK OLIVE TAPANADE

Spaghetti al limone
SPAGHETTI WITH LEMON

Filetto alla Garga con funghi porcini
FILET "GARGA" STYLE WITH PORCINI

Crostini all'olive nere
TOASTS WITH BLACK OLIVE TAPANADE

Spaghetti al limone
SPAGHETTI WITH LEMON

Filetto alla Garga con funghi porcini
FILET "GARGA" STYLE WITH PORCINI

Crostini all'olive nere

TOASTS WITH BLACK OLIVE TAPANADE

"This is a very rich crostini and is sure to be loved by all lovers of olives!"

Ingredients

Extra virgin olive oil

Salt and black pepper
   to taste

Garlic, minced

Kalamata olives,
   pit removed

Dried tomatoes,
   rehydrated
   and chopped

Fresh basil, chopped

Crusty Italian bread,
   sliced to desired
   thickness

Method

Place the kalamata olives on a cutting board and finely chop. Place the chopped olives, dried tomatoes and basil in a bowl and drizzle in enough olive oil to moisten. Season to taste with salt and pepper, mix well and set aside. Now mix the remaining olive oil with the garlic and brush each slice of bread with this flavored oil.

Toast both sides until the edges of the bread begin to brown. Top each slice of the toasted bread with the olive mixture and serve.

Spaghetti al limone

SPAGHETTI WITH LEMON

Ingredients

12 ounces spaghetti

2 lemons, zest and juiced

3/4 cup parmesan,
   freshly grated

Salt and black pepper

6 large fresh basil
   leaves, chopped

Method

Cook the spaghetti in a generous amount of salted boiling water. Drain and reserve warm.

Meanwhile, in a bowl, whisk the lemon juice with the olive oil, then add the parmesan cheese and mix until thick and creamy.

Add the sauce to the hot spaghetti and mix well. Fold in the chopped basil and chopped lemon zest and serve on warm plates.

Filetto alla Garga con funghi porcini

FILET "GARGA" STYLE WITH PORCINI

"This wonderful dish was created for us by the incredible Chef Giuliano Gargani in his wonderful Florentine trattoria, GARGA. The steak and mushroom resemble an enormous American hamburger and tastes like heaven."

Ingredients

Two-8 ounce beef filets

2 large, fresh porcini or
   portabello mushroom
   caps

2 ounces fresh arugula
   greens, chopped

6 lemon wedges

Salt and black pepper

Olive oil

Method

Preheat your char grill. Gently pound the filets, with the back of a pan, to flatten to a thickness of 2 inches. Season both sides of the filets with salt, pepper and olive oil. Season both sides of the mushroom caps with salt, pepper and olive oil.

Grill the filets on the hottest spot of your grill, turning often. At the same time grill the mushroom caps on a less hot spot of your grill, also turning often.

The filets should cook for 3 to 4 minutes on each side, for medium rare, then remove from the grill and let rest while the mushrooms finish cooking. Once the mushrooms are cooked, 3-4 minutes per side, remove from the heat, let rest at room temperature for 10 minutes

Reheat the filets on both sides on the hot spot of your grill for 1-2 minutes and serve with the mushrooms caps on top of the filets. Garnish with arugula greens, lemon wedges, black pepper and olive oil.

COURTNEY AND MILES JAMES
DOING RESEARCH IN FLORENCE

"But the wild things cried, 'Oh please don't go -
we'll eat you up - we love you so!'"

WHERE THE WILD THINGS ARE by MAURICE SENDAK, 1963

Insalata di pepperoni gialle capperi
YELLOW PEPPER SALAD WITH CAPERS

Carciofi fritti con limone e olio
CARCIOFI FRITTI WITH PARSLEY, LEMON AND OLIVE OIL

Pollo arrosto
ROASTED ROSEMARY CHICKEN

Insalata di pepperoni gialli e capperi
YELLOW PEPPER SALAD WITH CAPERS

Carciofi fritti con limone ed olio
FRIED ARTICHOKES WITH PARSLEY, LEMON AND OLIVE OIL

Pollo arrosto
ROASTED ROSEMARY CHICKEN

Carciofi fritti con limone ed olio

FRIED ARTICHOKE HEARTS
WITH PARSLEY, LEMON AND
OLIVE OIL

"The simplicity of this dish is elegant and pure. The wonderful flavor of artichokes are heightened by the lemon peel, raw garlic and parsley."

Ingredients

4 artichokes

The peel of one lemon

1 peeled garlic clove

1 bunch Italian parsley,
leaves only

Extra-virgin olive oil

Salt and black pepper

Freshly grated
parmesan

3 cups peanut oil
for frying

Artichoke Preparation

Cut the artichokes in half and remove the choke. Slice the artichokes into 1/8 inch slices and reserve in a bowl. Squeeze the peeled lemon over the slices.

Method

In a heavy-bottomed pan, heat the peanut oil to 375 degrees. Using a knife or mezzaluna, chop the parsley, garlic and lemon peel to a fine mince. Fry the slices of artichokes until golden

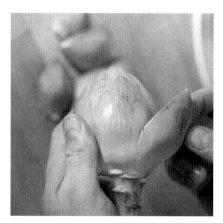

brown. Remove onto paper towels and season with salt and pepper. Divide the fried artichoke slices onto two warm appetizer plates and sprinkle with the chopped lemon peel, garlic and parsley. Add a splash of extra-virgin olive oil and a sprinkle of parmesan over the top. Serve immediately.

Insalata di pepperoni gialli e capperi

YELLOW PEPPER SALAD WITH CAPERS

Ingredients

1 large ripe yellow
   tomato
1 clove garlic, peeled
   and thinly sliced
5 fresh basil leaves,
   torn into thirds
12 to 14 fresh mint
   leaves
1/4 cup olive oil
4 large yellow bell
   peppers

2 tablespoons capers
Salt and black pepper

Method

Purée the tomato and pass through a sieve into a mixing bowl. Season the tomato mixture with salt and pepper. Add the basil, olive oil and 5 mint leaves. Mix very well, cover and refrigerate for an hour. Meanwhile roast the peppers over an open flame on your stove top or char grill them until the skins blister and turn black. Once the skins are blistered and charred, place the peppers in a plastic bag and refrigerate for 20 minutes. Remove the peppers from the bag and peel them. Open the peppers, remove the stem and seeds and cut into thin strips. Add the cleaned pepper strips to the tomato marinade and let stand at room temperature for 20 minutes. Arrange on a serving plate or bowl and garnish with remaining mint leaves and capers.

Pollo arrosto

ROASTED ROSEMARY CHICKEN

Ingredients

One 2 pound fresh chicken
   (we recommend
   free range if possible)
2 ounces fresh
   rosemary
Olive oil
Salt and pepper
1 lemon

Method

Preheat your oven to 350 degrees Fahrenheit. Season the inside and outside of the chicken with salt and pepper. Stuff the rosemary inside the chicken and under the skin of the breast.

Cut the lemon in half and place in the chicken next to the rosemary. Pour some olive oil over the top and put the chicken in a roasting pan. Bake uncovered for 1 hour, or until the chicken is fully cooked.

Remove from the heat and let rest for 5 minutes. Carefully cut the chicken in half and divide onto 2 dinner plates. Season with salt, pepper and olive oil. Serve immediately.

"Her dark hair was scattered
and its beauty stung his eyes like smoke
and ate into his heart."

DOCTOR ZHIVAGO by BORIS PASTERNAK, 1958

Zuppa di pomodori e pepperoni gialli con aragosta ed olio di basilico
YELLOW TOMATO AND PEPPER SOUP WITH LOBSTER AND BASIL OIL

Pollo al limone
CHICKEN WITH LEMON

Nidi di erbucce
SAUTEED SPINACH AND FRIED EGG NESTS

Zuppa di pomodori e pepperoni gialli con aragosta ed olio di basilico
YELLOW TOMATO AND PEPPER SOUP WITH LOBSTER AND BASIL OIL

Pollo al limone
CHICKEN WITH LEMON

Nidi di erbucce
SAUTEED SPINACH AND FRIED EGG NESTS

Zuppa di pomodori e peperoni gialli con aragosto e olio di basilico

YELLOW TOMATO AND PEPPER
SOUP WITH LOBSTER
AND BASIL OIL

"The intense yellow of this soup is likened to a yellow Ferrari screaming through the wine country of Tuscany. Both wild and rare, this soup with its delicate lobster and intense basil oil will enrapture you"

Ingredients

2 large yellow peppers,
  cored, seeded and
  quartered

2 ripe yellow tomatoes,
  cored and quartered

1 medium cucumber,
  peeled, seeded, and
  chopped

2 peeled garlic cloves

2 ounces champagne
  or white wine vinegar

1/2 pound steamed
  lobster tail

2 bunches fresh basil
  leaves

2 cups extra-virgin olive oil

Salt and black pepper

Method

In a blender, add the yellow peppers, tomatoes, cucumbers, garlic, 1/4 of the basil, 1/2 cup of the olive oil and vinegar. Season with salt and pepper and purée. Transfer to a bowl and refrigerate. Rinse and dry the blender, then add the remaining basil and olive oil and purée. Pass the basil oil through a piece of cheesecloth catching the infused, green basil oil in a bowl below. Slice the steamed and chilled lobster tail into 8 pieces and place in the bottom of 2 chilled bowls. Ladle the chilled soup around the lobster and sprinkle the basil oil over the top. Garnish with fresh basil leaves.

Pollo al limone

CHICKEN WITH LEMON

"This dish can be prepared when you're on the run or have an important date. If you have time you can marinate the bird overnight in the refrigerator. The longer you let it marinate the better it gets."

Ingredients

One-3 to 4 pound
  chicken cut into
  quarters

4 lemons

1/2 cup olive oil

4 sprigs fresh rosemary

4 peeled cloves garlic,
  sliced

Salt and black pepper

Method

Preheat the oven to 350 degrees. Cut the lemons in half and squeeze all the juice into a bowl. Stuff the lemon rinds and rosemary inside the chicken. Mix the olive oil and garlic with the lemon juice and season with salt and pepper. Marinate the chicken for 2 to 3 hours, turning occasionally in the marinade. Remove the chicken from the marinade and place in a baking dish.

Bake for 45 minutes or until the juices run clear. Turn the chicken several times while baking. Once done, place the bird under a hot broiler to crisp and color the skin.

Nidi di erbucce

SAUTEED SPINACH AND FRIED EGG NESTS

Ingredients

2 pounds fresh spinach

2 garlic cloves, minced

4 tablespoons olive oil

6 eggs

Salt and black pepper

Method

Preheat your oven to 350 degrees Fahrenheit.

In a large skillet over medium heat, warm half of the olive oil. Add spinach and garlic, sauté gently, stirring until tender. Season with salt and pepper, remove from pan onto a plate and let cool at room temperature. Once cooled, squeeze out any excess moisture. Divide cooled spinach into 6 equal portions and roll each portion into a firm ball. With your fingertip, make a hollow in the center of each ball to form a nest-like indention. Brush a baking dish with remaining olive oil and arrange spinach in it, hollow side up. Crack one egg into each of the hollows and bake "nests" for 10 minutes or until eggs are solidified. Season with salt and pepper.

"She smelled like apple blossoms, but then she always did."

THE STORY OF HENRI TOD by WILLIAM F. BUCKLEY, 1984

Fiori di zucchini fritti
FRIED ZUCCHINI BLOSOMS

Orecchiette all'arrabiata
ORCCHIETTE WITH TOMATO, GARLIC, BACON, CAPERS AND MUSHROOMS

Trota al tartufo
TROUT WITH TRUFFLES

Fiori di zucchini fritti
FRIED ZUCCHINI BLOSSOMS

Orechiette all'arabbiata
ORCCHIETTE WITH TOMATO, GARLIC, BACON, CAPERS AND MUSHROOMS

Trote al tartufo
TROUT WITH TRUFFLES

Fiori di zucchini fritti

STUFFED ZUCCHINI BLOSSOMS

Ingredients

16 zucchini blossoms

3 ounces freshly grated mozzarella

3 ounces freshly grated parmesan

1 ounce bread crumbs

Olive oil

Salt and black pepper

1 sprig fresh rosemary leaves, chopped

1 cup all-purpose flour

1 cup soda water

1 large egg

1 quart peanut oil for frying

Method

In a large heavy-bottomed frying pan, heat the peanut oil to 350 degrees Fahrenheit. In a large mixing bowl, combine the soda water, flour and egg with a whisk. Season with salt and pepper and let stand at room temperature until needed. Carefully remove

the stamen from inside the blossoms. Brush away any dirt or insects from the inside and outside of the blossoms using a soft brush and never any water! In a mixing bowl, combine the mozzarella, parmesan and bread crumbs. Add a tablespoon of olive oil and season with salt, pepper and rosemary.

Continue mixing until the cheese combines with the oil and seasonings. Stuff the cleaned blossoms with the cheese mixture and place the stuffed blossoms in the batter. Make sure the batter is coating the entire blossom and carefully slip the battered blossoms into the hot oil one at a time. Repeat this process being careful not to overcrowd the frying pan. Remove the golden brown squash blossoms onto absorbent paper towels and season with salt and pepper. Serve immediately.

Orecchiette all'arrabbiata

ORECCHIETTE WITH TOMATO, GARLIC, BACON, CAPERS AND MUSHROOMS

"This is our untraditional version of a favorite!"

Ingredients

12 ounces orecchiette
    pasta

5 roma or plum
    tomatoes, skin
    removed

3 cloves garlic, peeled
    and rough chopped

5 strips peppered
    bacon or pancetta,
    chopped

1 tablespoon capers

1 1/2 cups chopped
    porcini or portabello
    mushrooms

1 teaspoon red
    chile flakes

1 tablespoon chopped
    Italian parsley

Freshly grated
    parmesan cheese

Method

In a heavy-bottomed sauce pan, gently cook the bacon until golden brown and starting to crisp. Remove the bacon from the pan onto absorbent paper towels and add the garlic to the hot pan with bacon drippings. Brown the garlic and add the mushrooms.

Cook over high heat until the mushrooms are tender. Add the cooked bacon, chile flakes, tomatoes and capers to the pan and season with salt and pepper.

Cook uncovered simmering for 20 minutes or until the sauce has thickened. Meanwhile cook the orecchiette in a generous amount of salted boiling water until tender. Drain the pasta and toss with the cooked tomato sauce. Garnish with chopped parsley and parmesan cheese.

Trote
al tartufo

TROUT WITH TRUFFLES

Ingredients

2 cleaned trout, 1/2 to
    3/4 pound each, head
    and tail on

2 tablespoons olive oil

1 ounce fresh white
    truffle slices

Truffle oil

1/4 cup bread crumbs

1/4 cup chopped Italian
    parsley

Salt and black pepper

Edible flowers (page 135)

Method

Preheat your char grill.

In a mixing bowl, combine the bread crumbs with the truffle oil and truffle slices and season with salt and pepper.

Stuff the truffled bread crumbs into the cavities of the trout. Season the outside of the trout with salt, pepper and olive oil.

Place the stuffed trout on the hot spot of your grill and cook turning once or twice on each side for 4 to 5 minutes or until the fish is charred and cooked through.

Garnish with chopped parsley and edible flowers.

"The hand stroked her face softly, softly,
with infinite soothing and assurance and, at last,
there was the soft touch of a kiss on the cheek."

LADY CHATTERLY'S LOVER by D. H. LAWRENCE, 1928

Insalata caprese
FRESH MOZZARELLA, TOMATO AND BASIL SALAD

Tonnaccio al pesto e vinagrette
GRILLED TUNA WITH PESTO VINAIGRETTE

Risotto agli asparagi
ASPARAGUS RICE

Insalata caprese
FRESH MOZZARELLA, TOMATO AND BASIL SALAD

Tonnaccio al pesto e vinagrette
GRILLED TUNA WITH PESTO VINAIGRETTE

Risotto agli asparagi
ASPARAGUS RICE

Insalata caprese

FRESH MOZZARELLA, TOMATO
AND BASIL SALAD

Ingredients

2 vine ripened red
   tomatoes
2 fresh buffalo
   mozzarella balls
12 fresh basil leaves
Salt and black pepper
Olive oil

Method

Slice the tomatoes and mozzarella and season with salt and pepper. Layer the tomato and mozzarella slices with the basil leaves. Drizzle some olive oil over the top and season with salt and pepper.

Tonnaccio al pesto e vinagrette

GRILLED TUNA WITH A MARINADE OF PESTO VINAIGRETTE

"The pesto can be made as a base and stored in the refrigerator or it can be frozen for as long as you need. It can be served with many dishes like pasta, fish, veal,chicken, shellfish or salads. When the basil plants in the garden go wild it's time to make a big batch of pesto!"

Ingredients

2 - 8 ounce sushi quality
   tuna steaks
3 ripe plum tomatoes,
   cut in half, seeded
   and diced
2 ounces red wine vinegar
1 recipe of pesto
   (page 119 for recipe)
Olive oil
Salt and black pepper
5 or 6 large basil leaves

Method

To make the vinaigrette combine the pesto, vinegar and tomatoes. Season with salt, pepper and olive oil. Season the tuna steaks on all sides with salt, pepper, and olive oil. Grill over an open flame for 2 to 3 minutes on both sides. Cut into thin slices and divide the tuna between two warm dinner plates. Top with the pesto vinaigrette, black pepper, fresh basil and olive oil.

Risotto agli asparagi

RICE WITH ASPARAGUS

Ingredients

2 1/2 cups homemade
   chicken stock
   (see page 133
   for recipe)
1/2 pound fresh asparagus
1/2 stick plus 2 tablespoons
   unsalted butter
2 ounces fresh spinach
   leaves
1 small white onion,
   peeled and chopped
1/4 cup dry white wine
1/4 cup vegetable
   stock (page 133 for
   recipe)

1 heaping cup arborio rice

Freshly grated

    parmesan cheese

Olive oil

Salt and black pepper

Method

Cut the asparagus in half and roughly chop the bottoms. Sauté the bottoms of the asparagus in a heavy-bottomed sauté pan with a splash of olive oil and half of the onion. When the onions become translucent, add the spinach, 1/2 stick of butter and vegetable stock. Bring to a boil and season with salt and pepper. Transfer the ingredients to a blender and purée. Pass the puréed asparagus butter through a sieve and reserve warm. Heat the chicken stock. Sauté the remaining onions with the remaining butter in a heavy-bottomed sauté pan. Once the onions are translucent, add the rice and stir so every grain is coated. Sauté for 1 to 2 minutes, stirring constantly, then add the wine and reduce until the wine is absorbed. Stir in enough of the hot chicken stock to just cover the rice. Stir and reduce the stock completely, then add a little more stock and repeat this process adding small amounts of stock and reducing the stock until the rice is tender and creamy but still a little firm in the middle, about 10 minutes. While hot, stir in the asparagus tips and the asparagus butter and continue to cook for 1 to 2 more minutes. Stir in some parmesan cheese and serve immediately.

"You'll find the bright places where Boom Bands are playing."

OH, THE PLACES YOU'LL GO! by DR. SUESS, 1990

Fettuccine al pesto con patate e fagiolini
FETTUCCINE WITH POTATOES, GREEN BEANS, AND PESTO

Cozze e vongole in guazzetto
MUSSELS AND CLAMS SERVED LIVORNO STYLE

Schiacciata al rosmarino
ROSEMARY FLAT BREAD

Fettuccine al pesto con patate e fagiolini
FETTUCCINE WITH POTATOES, GREEN BEANS, AND PESTO

Cozze e vongole stufate in guazzetto
MUSSELS AND CLAMS STEWED LIVORNO STYLE

Schiacciata al sambuco
ROSEMARY FLAT BREAD

Fettuccine al pesto con patate e fagiolini

FETTUCCINE WITH PESTO, POTATOES AND GREEN BEANS

Ingredients

12 ounces fettuccine

1 medium potato

2 oz. fresh green beans

1 clove garlic, minced

Olive oil

1 cup fresh basil leaves

1 T pine nuts, toasted

Freshly grated

   parmesan cheese

Salt and black pepper

Method

For the pesto, put the garlic, 2 tablespoons olive oil, basil leaves and pine nuts in a food processor and puree to a thick sauce consistency. Season with salt and pepper and set aside. Peel the potatoes and cut them into small cubes. Trim off the ends of the green beans and cut them in half. Boil the potatoes in a generous amount of salted boiling water. When the potatoes are almost tender, add the pasta and green beans and cook for another 2 to 3 minutes. Drain the pasta and vegetables and toss with the pesto sauce. Garnish with fresh parmesan, black pepper and olive oil.

Cozze e vongole stufate in guazzetto

MUSSELS AND CLAMS STEWED LIVORNO STYLE

Ingredients

3/4 pound fresh

   cleaned small black

   mussels

3/4 pound fresh

   cleaned

   cherrystone clams

1 small carrot, peeled

1 small red onion,

   peeled

1 garlic clove, peeled

30 Italian parsley leaves

2 tablespoons olive oil

2 bay leaves

Salt and black pepper

1 pinch red chile flakes

1 cup dry white wine

4 large slices toasted

Tuscan bread

Method

Finely chop the carrot, onion, garlic and half the parsley all together on a cutting board. Heat the oil in a heavy-bottomed sauté pan and sauté the vegetables over medium high heat for ten minutes, continue stirring often with a wooden spoon. Add the bay leaves and season with salt, pepper and chile flakes. Add the wine and reduce it by half.

Once the wine has reduced add the mussels and clams and stir very well. Cook covered for 4 to 5 minutes or until the mussels and clams have steamed open. Remove and discard the bay leaves and the mussels and clams that have not opened. Using a slotted spoon, transfer the mussels and clams to a serving platter and reduce the sauce 1 minute more stirring constantly. Place the toasted Tuscan bread slices on 2 dinner plates and spoon the reduced sauce over each slice of the bread. Chop the other half of the parsley roughly and sprinkle over the bread slices. Pass the mussels and clams at the table with the bread.

Schiacciata al sambuco

ROSEMARY FLAT BREAD

Ingredients

2/3 cup water,

100 degrees Fahrenheit

1 ounce fresh yeast or

1 scant tablespoon

dry active yeast

2 1/2 cups all purpose flour

1/2 cup fresh chopped

rosemary leaves

2 tablespoons olive oil

Method

Place the warm water in a mixing bowl and stir in the yeast. Let stand for 10 minutes so the yeast will be fully dissolved and foamy. Mix the flour salt and rosemary in a mixing bowl with a whisk to incorporate. Heap the flour mixture on a work surface and make a well in the center.

Pour the dissolved yeast and water into the well. With a fork, gradually whisk in the

flour until all the liquid is absorbed and a soft dough forms. On a floured surface, knead the dough until it is soft and elastic, about 10 minutes. Shape into a ball and place in a floured bowl.

Cover and place in a warm spot in the kitchen for 1 hour, or until doubled in size. Turn the risen dough onto a floured work surface. Punch the dough down and flatten the dough with the palms of your hands into a disc shape approximately 9 inches in diameter and 3/8 inch thick.

Dust a 9-inch cake pan with flour and place the dough disc in the pan. Let rise for 20 minutes. Meanwhile preheat your oven to 400 degrees Fahrenheit.

With your finger, make several shallow indentations on the surface of the dough and sprinkle with olive oil and salt. Bake for 30 minutes or until golden brown.

Remove from the oven and let cool for a few minutes, then turn onto a wire rack to let cool completely. Cut in wedges and serve with olive oil at room temperature.

"Fantasy love is better than reality love."

THE PHILOSOPHY OF ANDY WARHOL: A TO B AND BACK AGAIN, by ANDY WARHOL, 1977

LIVORNO MENU

Risotto con fiori di zucchini
RICE WITH ZUCCHINI FLOWERS

Vitello tonnato
VEAL WITH TUNA SAUCE

Insalata rucola con parmigiano reggiano
ARUGULA SALAD WITH PARMESAN RIBBONS

Risotto con fiori di zucchini
RICE WITH ZUCCHINI FLOWERS

Vitello tonnato
VEAL WITH TUNA SAUCE

Insalata rucola con parmigiano reggiano
ARUGULA SALAD WITH PARMESAN RIBBONS

Risotto con fiori di zucchini

RICE WITH ZUCCHINI FLOWERS

"This summer risotto is both beautiful and delicate. If you have lots of zucchini flowers you can slice them and add them raw to the top of the finished dish for a more sensual presentation."

Ingredients

6 large zucchini flowers

3 small young zucchini

2 cups homemade
chicken stock (page
133 for recipe)

5 tablespoons unsalted
butter

1 tablespoon olive oil

1 small white onion,
peeled & chopped

1 cup arborio or
carnarola rice

1/2 cup dry white wine

1 cup parmesan grated

5 or 6 large basil
leaves, thinly sliced

Salt and black pepper

Prepare the risotto

Remove the spiky petals on the outside of the flower. Cut each flower vertically into 4 pieces. Brush to get rid of any dirt or insects, but do not wash it. Slice the whole zucchini into thin discs. Heat the chicken stock and season to taste with salt and pepper. Melt four tablespoons butter and all the olive oil in a heavy-bottomed casserole. Sauté the onion until soft and translucent. Add the rice and stir so that every grain is coated, approximately one minute. Add 2 or so ladles full of hot stock to the rice and simmer stirring until the rice has absorbed nearly all the liquid. Continue to add more stock as the previous addition is absorbed. After about 15 minutes, add first the zucchini discs, then the flower strands, along with the last few ladles of stock. The zucchini should have a little bite, the flowers will disappear and the rice will have a creamy coating but will remain al dente. Add the remaining butter and season to taste with salt, black pepper, parmesan and basil. Garnish the top with extra slices of zucchini flowers if possible.

Vitello Tonnato

VEAL WITH TUNA SAUCE

Ingredients

One 3/4 pound
veal roast

All-purpose flour

1 tablespoon olive oil

1 peeled garlic clove

Salt and black pepper

1/4 dry white wine

1 ounce unsalted
butter

1/2 cup vegetable
broth (page 133 for
recipe)

Tuna sauce

3 ounces olive oil-packed
canned tuna

1 teaspoon anchovy paste

1 tablespoon
vegetable broth
(page 133 for recipe)

1 tablespoon capers,

   plus extra for garnish

1/4 cup mayonnaise

Method

Preheat the oven to 375 degrees.

For the roast

Tie the roast with kitchen string, season with salt and black pepper and lightly dust with flour. Brown the roast in a heavy-bottomed sauté pan with the oil and garlic. Once the meat is golden brown on all sides, add the wine and continue cooking until the wine almost evaporates. Place the butter in the pan and roast in the oven for 20 to 30 minutes, or until cooked throughout.

Check the broth in the pan while the meat is roasting, and add some vegetable broth if liquid has evaporated. Once the meat is

cooked, remove from the heat and let cool. This part of the recipe may be done 1 day in advance. Cover and refrigerate overnight.

For the sauce

Place the drained tuna, anchovy paste, broth, and the capers in a food processor. Purée the ingredients to a creamy consistency. Put the mayonnaise in a mixing bowl and add the processed tuna mixture, mixing well with a rubber spatula. Cut the cold roasted veal into thin slices and arrange on two dinner plates. Spread the tuna sauce over the meat and garnish with extra capers. Serve chilled.

Insalata rucola con parmigiano

ARUGULA SALAD WITH
PARMESAN RIBBONS

Ingredients

6 ounces fresh arugula

6 parmesan ribbons

Extra-virgin olive oil

Salt and black pepper

Fresh lemon slices, and

   one lemon for juice

Method

Wash and dry the fresh arugula. In a bowl, mix equal parts of olive oil and lemon juice together with a whisk.

Season with salt and pepper. Dress the arugula greens with the oil and lemon mixture and divide onto two salad plates.

Divide the parmesan ribbons. The ribbons are cut from a block of parmesan cheese with a vegetable peeler. Over the top of the dressed greens and sprinkle with more black pepper.

"When he took her in his arms, she turned her body to meet his straight on, to feel the width of his chest with the width or hers, the length of his legs with the length of hers, as if she were lying against him, and her feet felt no weight, and she was held upright by the pressure of his body."

THE FOUNTAINHEAD by AYN RAND, 1943

Panzanella
TOMATO BREAD SALAD

Dorado arrosto
ROASTED DORADO

Arrosto con patate, salvia e pancetta
ROASTED POTATOES, SAGE AND PANCETTA

Panzanella
TOMATO BREAD SALAD

Dorado arrosto
ROASTED DORADO

Arrosto con patate, salvia e pancetta
ROASTED POTATOES, SAGE AND PANCETTA

Panzanella

TOMATO AND BREAD SALAD

Ingredients

3 to 4 slices of stale
  Tuscan bread
  (page 68 for recipe)
4 fresh plum tomatoes
2 garlic cloves,crushed
  to a paste with salt
Salt and black pepper
Extra-virgin olive oil
3 tablespoons red wine
  vinegar
1 large red bell pepper
1 large yellow bell
  pepper
1/4 cup capers
10 anchovy filets
1/4 cup pitted
  black olives
1 bunch fresh basil

Method
Place the thick slices of stale bread in a bowl. Skin, halve, and seed the tomatoes into a strainer over another bowl to retain the tomato juice.

Season the juice with the garlic paste and some salt and pepper, then add a splash of olive oil and a few drops of red wine vinegar. Pour the seasoned tomato juices over the bread and toss until the bread has absorbed all the liquid.

If the bread seems to need more liquid, add more olive oil. Grill the peppers whole until blackened all over, then peel, seed and cut into eighths lengthwise. In a separate bowl soak the capers and the anchovy filets in enough red wine vinegar to cover.

In a medium size dish, lay the soaked bread in the bottom to line the dish and top with some of the remaining ingredients.

Continue with another layer of bread and other ingredients until all have been used. The final layer should have the peppers, tomatoes, capers, anchovies, olives, and basil all visible.

Rest for an hour at room temperature before serving with additional extra-virgin olive oil.

Dorado arrosto con patate, salvia e pancetta

ROASTED DORADO WITH
ROASTED POTATOES, SAGE
AND PANCETTA

Ingredients

One-1 1/2 pound
 dorado fish

1/2 ounces fresh rosemary

2 oz. fresh sage leaves

2 peeled garlic cloves,
 sliced

1 pound small yellow
 potatoes, peeled

4 ounces pancetta or
 bacon

Olive oil

Salt and black pepper

Method

Preheat the oven to 375 degrees Fahrenheit. Season the inside and outside of the fish with salt and pepper. Stuff the inside of the fish with the rosemary and half of the sage.

Set the fish aside at room temperature. Cut the yellow potatoes into quarters, lengthwise. Place in a roasting pan and coat with olive oil, salt and black pepper.

Toss in the rest of the sage and garlic. Cut the pancetta into thin slices and add to the roasting pan.

Make sure the sage and pancetta are distributed evenly. Place the fish on top of the potato mixture and pour a drizzle of olive oil over the top of the entire roasting pan.

Roast in the oven for 20 minutes covered with foil. Remove the foil and continue roasting for another 20 minutes, or until the fish is tender and flaky and the potatoes are golden brown and tender as well.

"It was not that she was afraid, she said, but that a strange feeling took hold of her every time the engine speed went to maximum revs."

ENZO FERRARI about ANNA MAGNANI, 1976

SAN STEFANO MENU

Fagioli con arugula, carciofi e parmigiano
BEANS WITH ARUGULA, ARTICHOKE AND PARMESAN

Spaghetti Vongole
SPAGHETTI WITH CLAMS

Torta alla pomodoro e basilico con insalate miste
TOMATO AND BASIL TART WITH BITTER GREENS /

Fagioli con rucola, carciofi e parmigiano
BEANS WITH ARUGULA, ARTICHOKE AND PARMESAN

Spaghetti vongole
SPAGHETTI WITH CLAMS

Torta alla pomodoro e basilico con insalate miste
TOMATO AND BASIL TART WITH BITTER GREENS

Fagioli con rucola, carciofi e parmigiano

WHITE BEANS WITH ARUGULA, ARTICHOKE AND SHAVED PARMESAN CHEESE

Ingredients for the white beans

1/2 cup white beans

1 small celery stalk

2 cloves peeled garlic

1 small peeled carrot

Salt

Additional ingredients

Arugula leaves

2 fresh artichoke hearts,

cleaned and

shaved vertically

(see page 92)

Shaved parmesan cheese

Salt and black pepper

Prepare the white beans

Soak the beans in a bowl of cold water overnight. The next day rinse the beans under cold running water and place them in a stock pot with 2 quarts cold water. Add the celery, garlic and carrots and bring to a simmer. Let the beans simmer for approximately 45 minutes or until tender.

You want the beans to be soft but still retain their shape. Add the salt and simmer 1 to 2 minutes more. Drain the beans. Place them in a bowl to cool and cover with moist paper towels.

To assemble
Dress the beans in the bowl you cooled them in with extra-virgin olive oil, salt and black pepper to taste. Divide the seasoned beans between two appetizer plates. Top the beans with the arugula, shaved artichokes and shaved parmesan. Drizzle more extra-virgin olive oil over the top and sprinkle more black pepper on as well.

Spaghetti vongole

SPAGHETTI WITH CLAMS

Ingredients

1 pound small fresh clams

2 tablespoons olive oil

1/2 cup dry white wine

2 garlic cloves, peeled

and sliced

6 ounces spaghetti

1 teaspoon red chile

flakes

1 tablespoon fresh

chopped parsley

1 roma tomato,

peeled, seeded

and diced

Salt and pepper

Method
Scrub the clam shells clean under running water, then soak in clean water. Continue to soak and change the water several times.

Heat the olive oil in a heavy-bottomed pan and add the wine, chile flakes and garlic. Add the clams and cook covered over high heat. Shake the covered pan almost constantly until the clams steam open, about 4 to 5 minutes. Remove and discard any clams that don't open. Reserve the steamed clams warm. Cook the spaghetti in a generous amount of boiling salted water. Drain and toss with the clams, tomatoes, parsley, salt and pepper. Serve on two warm plates immediately.

Torta alla pomodoro e basilico con insalate miste

TOMATO AND BASIL TART WITH PESTO DRESSED GREENS

For the crust

8 ounces all-purpose flour

4 ounces cold unsalted
    butter

Pinch of salt

Pinch of freshly grated
    nutmeg

5 tablespoons cold water

For the filling

1 small celery stalk,
    chopped

1 small carrot, peeled
    and chopped

1 small red onion,
    peeled & chopped

1 garlic clove, peeled
    and chopped

10 sprigs Italian parsley,
    leaves only, chopped

10 large basil
    leaves,chopped

1 1/2 pounds very ripe
    fresh tomatoes,
    chopped (save juice!)

2 tablespoons olive oil

2 tablespoons unsalted
    butter

Salt and black pepper to
    taste

3 extra large eggs

1/2 cup parmigiano
    reggiano

For the pesto

4 ounces fresh basil
    leaves

2 ounces toasted
    pine nuts

2 ounces extra-
virgin olive oil

Grated parmigiano
    reggiano

Salt and black pepper

Small handful clipped
    and cleaned spinach

Prepare the crust

Sift the flour onto a board and arrange it in a mound. cut the butter into pieces and place them over the mound. Use a metal dough scraper to incorporate the butter into the flour, adding the water 1 tablespoon at a time, and season with salt and nutmeg. When all the water is incorporated, a ball of dough should be formed. Place the ball in plastic wrap and refrigerate for 2 hours or overnight.

Prepare the filling

Place the fresh tomatoes in a heavy-bottomed non-reactive casserole, then arrange all the prepared vegetables over the tomatoes. Pour the olive oil over the top. Cover casserole, place over medium heat and cook for at least 1 hour. Don't stir but shake the

(recipe continues on page 132)

Sorbetto d'arance tarocchi
BLOOD ORANGE SORBET

Monte bianco
MERINGUE, CREAM AND CHESTNUT TORTE

Torta di polenta
POLENTA CAKE

Fragole, mirtilli e lampone con zabaione
FRESH BERRIES WITH TOASTED ZABAIONE

Tiramisu
ESPRESSO-SOAKED LADY FINGERS WITH RUM AND MARSCARPONE

Pesche gratinate con chianti classico
GRILLED PEACHES WITH CHIANTI CLASSICO

Sorbetto d'arance tarocchi
BLOOD ORANGE SORBET

Monte bianco
MERINGUE, CREAM AND CHESTNUT TORTE

Torta di polenta
POLENTA CAKE

Sorbetto d'arance tarocchi

BLOOD ORANGE SORBET

Ingredients

1/2 cup blood orange juice
concentrate

2 cups simple syrup

3 1/2 cups water

Method
Combine and freeze in an ice cream freezer. Garnish with slices of blood orange.

Monte bianco

MERINGUE,
CREAM AND
CHESTNUT TORTE

Ingredients

1 cup confectioners
sugar

3/4 cup finely ground
hazelnuts

3/4 cup finely ground
chestnuts or
chestnut paste

5 egg whites

1/4 cup granulated
sugar

Heavy whipping cream

Method
Preheat your oven to 250 degrees Fahrenheit.

In a mixing bowl combine the nuts and confectioners sugar. Using your electric mixer, whisk the whites until soft peaks occur. Add the granulated sugar. Whip until stiff peaks are formed. Transfer the stiff whipped egg whites to a large mixing bowl and fold in the nuts 1/3 at a time.

Spread the meringue onto non-stick baking sheets in disc shapes and bake in the preheated oven for 4 hours. Once the meringues are cooked and cooled whip heavy cream to stiff peaks and layer the cooked meringues with the whipped cream. Top with roasted hazelnuts and chestnut paste.

Torta di polenta

POLENTA CAKE

Ingredients
2 cups softened
butter
2 1/2 cups sugar
6 cups coarsely ground
almonds
2 teaspoons pure vanilla
extract
6 large eggs
Grated zest of
4 lemons
Juice of 1 lemon
2 cups polenta flour
1/2 tablespoon baking
powder
1/4 teaspoon salt

Method
Preheat the oven to 325 degrees Fahrenheit. Butter and flour a 12-inch cake pan that is 2 inches deep.

Beat the butter and sugar together until pale and light. Stir in the ground almonds and vanilla.

Beat in the eggs, one at a time. Fold in the lemon zest and lemon juice, the polenta flour, baking powder and salt.

Spoon into the prepared pan and bake in the preheated oven for 45-50 minutes or until set. The cake will be deep brown on top.

Fragole, mirtilli e lampone con zabaione
FRESH BERRIES WITH TOASTED ZABAIONE

Tiramisu
ESPRESSO-SOAKED LADY FINGERS WITH RUM AND MARSCARPONE

Pesche gratinate con chianti classico
GRILLED PEACHES WITH CHIANTI CLASSICO

Fragole, mirtilli e lampone con zabaione

FRESH BERRIES WITH TOASTED ZABAIONE

Ingredients

8 ounces of your favorite berries (strawberries, blueberries, blackberries, raspberries)

3 large egg yolks

3 tablespoons sugar

1/3 cup sweet white wine

1 cup heavy cream

1 tablespoon confectioners sugar

Fresh mint for garnish

Method

In your electric mixer, whisk the yolks with granulated sugar until pale yellow. Add the sweet wine and set over a double boiler. Whisk constantly and cook until thickened and pale white in color. Set the mixing bowl in an ice bath to cool off. In another mixing bowl, whisk the heavy cream and confectioners sugar to stiff peaks. Fold the cream into the cooled zabaione. arrange the fruit on a plate and top with a dollop of the zabaione and toast with a torch. Garnish with fresh mint and serve immediately.

Tiramisu

ESPRESSO-SOAKED LADY FINGERS WITH RUM AND MARSCARPONE

Ingredients

4 teaspoons dark rum

1/2 pound mascarpone cheese

1 1/2 cups strong espresso, cooled

24 Italian lady fingers, toasted

1 1/2 tablespoons white sugar

3 egg yolks

Dark bittersweet chocolate for shaving

Method

Toast the ladyfingers in a preheated 375 degrees Fahrenheit oven for 15 minutes or until dried. Beat the egg yolks and the sugar until very light. Beat in 2 teaspoons of the rum, and then beat in the mascarpone until the mixture is smooth. Beat in 2 teaspoons of the espresso until everything is well mixed. Add the remaining rum to the remaining espresso and dip each lady finger into it—be careful not to soak them or they will fall apart. Make a layer of ladyfingers in the bottom of a baking dish. Spoon the mascarpone mixture over the ladyfingers, cover with plastic wrap, and refrigerate for at least 30 minutes. Sprinkle the top with chocolate shavings and cut into squares before serving.

Pesche gratinate con chianti classico

GRILLED PEACHES WITH CHIANTI CLASSICO

Ingredients

3 ripe white peaches

1 Tahitian vanilla bean

2 tablespoons white sugar

1/2 cup Chianti Classico

2 tablespoons créme fraîche

Fresh mint leaves

(continued on page 130)

Granita di caffé con panna
COFFEE ICE WITH WHIPPED CREAM

Torta alle albicocche
APRICOT CAKE

Torta della nonna
GRANDMOTHER'S CAKE

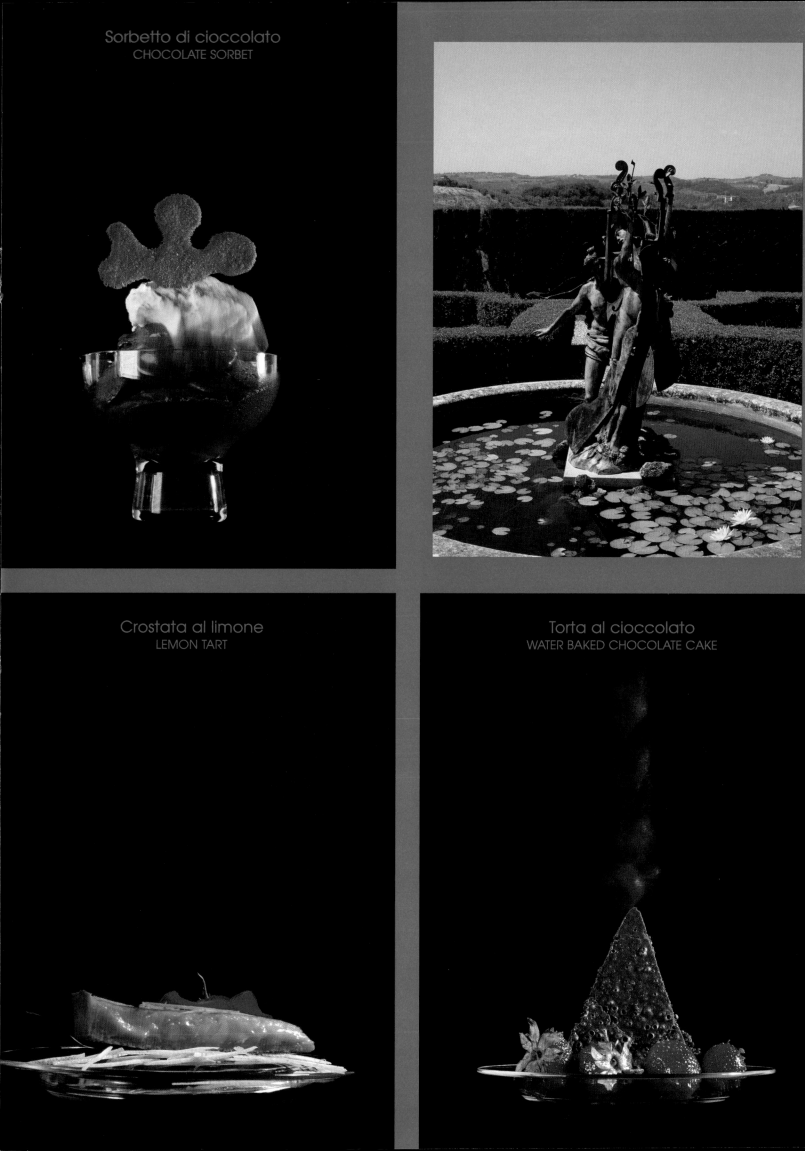

Sorbetto di cioccolato
CHOCOLATE SORBET

Crostata al limone
LEMON TART

Torta al cioccolato
WATER BAKED CHOCOLATE CAKE

Granita di caffé con panna
COFFEE ICE WITH WHIPPED CREAM

Torta alle albicocche
APRICOT CAKE

Torta al cioccolato
WATER BAKED CHOCOLATE CAKE

Granita di caffé con panna

Coffee ice
with whipped cream

Ingredients

12 ounces cold sweetened
espresso
Heavy cream

Method

Put the espresso in a cake pan and place in the freezer. Flake with a fork every half hour until completely frozen and flaky. Whip the cream to stiff peaks. Layer the granita and cream in a glass and serve with a spoon immediately.

Torta alle albicocche

APRICOT CAKE

"One of my favorite all time desserts, you can find on many Tuscan menus when the apricots are ripe and in abundance."

Ingredients

1/2 pound frozen puff
pastry, thawed
1 1/2 pound ripe fresh
apricots, cut in half, pitted
1/4 cup sugar
2 large eggs
1 teaspoon vanilla extract
2 teaspoons cornstarch
3/4 cup heavy cream
1/2 cup plain yogurt
or créme fraîche
Confectioners
sugar for dusting

Method

Preheat the oven to 375 degrees Fahrenheit. Line a 9-inch cake pan with parchment paper. Roll out the pastry and cut it into a 10-inch circle. Fit the puff pastry in the pan. Prick bottom in several places with a fork and place the apricot halves on it, cut side down, completely covering the pastry. Sprinkle with 1 tablespoon of sugar. Bake in the preheated for 15 minutes. Meanwhile, gently beat the eggs with remanning sugar and vanilla. Dissolve the cornstarch in the cream.

Add the yogurt and pour this mixture into the egg and sugar batter. Remove the pan from the oven and press the pastry down with your fingertips if it puffed up during cooking. Pour in the batter and return to the oven for 40 minutes, covering the cake after 10 minutes with foil. Remove from the oven and cool. Dust with sifted confectioners sugar before serving.

Torta al cioccolato

WATER BAKED
CHOCOLATE CAKE

Ingredients

10 eggs
3 cups sugar
1 1/2 pounds bittersweet
chocolate, chopped
into small pieces
2 cups unsalted butter

Method

Preheat the oven to 325 degrees. Line a 12-inch cake pan that is 2 inches deep with wax paper, then grease and flour it.

(continued on page 130)

Sorbetto di cioccolato
CHOCOLATE SORBET

Crostata al limone
LEMON TART

Torta della nonna
GRANDMOTHER'S CAKE

Sorbetto di cioccolato

CHOCOLATE SORBET

Ingredients

6 cups water

6 ounces sugar

5 ounces cocoa powder

1 pound bittersweet
    chocolate, chopped

Method

In a heavy-bottomed sauce pan, bring the water and sugar to a boil, stir in cocoa powder. Cook on low for 25 to 30 minutes. Pour over the chopped chocolate and stir until melted. Cool and freeze in an ice cream machine.

Crostata di limone

LEMON TART

Ingredients
For the pastry dough

2 1/2 cups all-purpose flour

A pinch of salt

1 cup unsalted cold butter

cut into cubes

1 scant cup
    confectioners sugar

3 large egg yolks

Method

Pulse the flour, salt and butter in a food processor until the mixture resembles coarse bread crumbs. Add the sugar, then the egg yolks, and pulse. The mixture will immediately combine and leave the sides of the bowl. Remove, wrap in plastic wrap, and chill for one hour.

Preheat oven to 350 degrees Fahrenheit. Coarsely grate the chilled pastry into your tart pan, then press it evenly onto the sides and bottom. Bake for 20 minutes or until very light brown. Remove the tart shell from the oven and leave to cool.

For the filling

7 lemons, zested and juiced

1 3/4 cups granulated sugar

6 large whole eggs

9 egg yolks

1 1/4 sticks unsalted butter,
    softened

Method

Raise the oven temperature to 450 degrees Fahrenheit. In a large heavy-bottomed saucepan, add all the ingredients except the butter and whisk until the eggs have broken up and the sugar has dissolved. Add half the butter and continue to whisk until the mixture begins to thicken and will coat the back of a spoon. Add the remaining butter and continue stirring until the mixture becomes very thick. Remove from the heat and rapidly cool over an ice bath, stirring often. Spoon the cooled lemon mixture into the baked tart shell and bake until the top browns, about 5 to 8 minutes.

Torta della nonna

GRANDMOTHER'S CAKE

Ingredients

For the custard

2 egg yolks

1/3 cup all-purpose flour

2 cups whole milk

1/2 cup sugar

(continued on page 131)

GRILLED PEACHES
(continued from page 125)

Method

Preheat oven 375 degrees Fahrenheit. Preheat your charcoal grill. Slice peaches in half and remove pits, trying to keep the cuts as clean as possible. Carefully place peach halves on grill, cut side down, and grill until each half becomes slightly charred. Thinly slice the vanilla bean lengthwise and scrape out the inside with a knife. Mix the scraped vanilla bean and the sugar in a bowl, using the back of a spoon. Place grilled peach halves face-up in a baking dish. Scatter the vanilla sugar over the peaches and pour in some Chianti Classico. Place in the preheated oven and bake for 10 minutes, or until the peaches are soft. Pour over the remaining Chianti Classico and serve hot or cold, with créme fraîche.

WATER BAKED CHOCOLATE CAKE
(continued from page 128)

Beat the eggs with 1/3 of the sugar until the volume quadruples. This will take at least 10 minutes in an electric mixer. Heat the remaining sugar in a pan with 1 cup water until the sugar has completely dissolved into a syrup. Place the chocolate and butter in the hot syrup and stir to combine. Remove from the heat and allow to cool slightly. Add the warm syrup to the eggs and continue to beat, on a more gentle speed, until completely combined—no more than about 20 seconds. Pour into the cake pan and place in a bain-marie of hot water. To ensure cake cooks evenly, the water should come up to the rim of the pan. Bake in the oven for 3 hours, or until set. Test by placing the flat of your hand gently on the surface. Leave to cool in the pan before unmolding.

GRANDMOTHER'S CAKE
(continued from page 129)

Method

In a heavy-bottomed sauce pan, combine the custard ingredients and cook over medium heat, whisking constantly, until thickened. Cool and reserve until later.

For the dough

1 1/2 cups corn meal

3/4 cup all-purpose flour

1/3 cup sugar

1 1/2 teaspoons baking powder

6 ounces unsalted butter

2 large eggs

2 egg yolks

Method

In an electric mixer, combine the dry ingredients and mix well. Add the eggs and mix until the dough comes together. Chill for one hour before rolling out. On a work surface, divide the dough and roll out to 1/8 inch thickness. Place the first half of the dough into a prepared 9-inch cake pan, covering the bottom and sides. Spread the custard onto the first layer of dough, then top with the other piece of dough and crimp the edges together. Top with toasted pine nuts and brush with an egg wash. Bake in the preheated oven for 20 to 25 minutes or until golden brown and cooked through.

TOMATO AND BASIL TART WITH PESTO DRESSED GREENS

(continued from page 121)

casserole to be sure the tomatoes do not stick to the bottom of the pan. (This is the way Mamma Rossa makes her sauce so I dare not question, unless I want the wooden spoon cracked over my knuckles.) Pass the contents of the casserole through the small hole disc of a food mill. Add the butter and season with salt and pepper.

Add the sauce back to the casserole and cook over medium heat for 15 minutes or until a thick sauce forms. Transfer the thick sauce to a bowl and cool completely. Butter 2 individual tart shells with teflon lining or removable bottoms. Flour a pastry board. Unwrap the pastry and knead it for about 30 seconds on the board, then use a rolling pin to roll the dough to desired thickness.

Cut the dough slightly larger than your tart shells, then gently press the dough into the bottom of the pan. Using a fork, make several punctures in the pastry to keep it from puffing up. Fit a piece of aluminum foil loosely over the pastry, then put dried beans over the foil to keep the pastry flat. Refrigerate the pastry for 1/2 hour. Place tart pan in a preheated 375 degree oven and bake for 15 minutes. Remove the pan from the oven, lift out the foil and beans, return the pan to the oven and bake until the crust is golden brown, about 5 to 7 minutes. In the meantime, finish preparing the filling by adding the eggs and parmesan cheese to the cooled sauce.

Season with salt and pepper to taste, and mix very well with a wooden spoon. Remove the tart pan from the oven (leaving the oven on). Let the tart shell cool for 15 minutes, then pour the filling in the crust. Bake the tart for 20 minutes longer.

Remove the pan from the oven and let cool for 15 minutes. Prepare the pesto: Place all the ingredients into a food processor and purée to a smooth consistency. Season to taste with salt and pepper. If you like your pesto a little thicker, then add a little more parmigiano.

Brodo di Pollo

HOMEMADE CHICKEN STOCK

Ingredients

2 chicken carcasses,
   roasted or raw

1 small white onion, peeled
   and quartered

2 medium carrots,
   peeled and chopped

4 celery stalks, chopped

3 peeled garlic cloves

The stems of 2 bunches
   of Italian parsley

4 sprigs fresh thyme

Salt and cracked
   black pepper

Method

Put the chicken carcasses into a large saucepan, cover with 3 quarts of cold water and bring to a boil. Skim the scum as it comes to the surface. Once the scum is removed add the rest of the ingredients and season with salt and pepper. Lower the heat so the stock can simmer gently for 1 1/2 hours, all the while skimming any scum that rises to the top. Strain, check season-

Brodo di pollo
HOMEMADE CHICKEN STOCK

Brodo di verdure
HOMEMADE VEGETABLE STOCK

Brodo di vitello
HOMEMADE VEAL STOCK

Pasta semolina
SEMOLINA PASTA

ing, and cool immediately. If not using immediately, refrigerate for no more than 2 days or freeze.

Brodo di verdure

HOMEMADE VEGETABLE STOCK

Ingredients

1/4 cup butter

2 medium onions, diced

3 medium carrots, diced

1 celery stalk, diced

1 head of lettuce, diced

2 large tomatoes quartered

1 bay leaf

10 sprigs parsley

10 peppercorns, crushed

1 sprig thyme

2 garlic cloves, diced

2 quarts boiling water

1 teaspoon salt

(any vegetables you might
   have, add diced)

Method
Add the first five ingredients plus any extra diced vegetables you might have to a deep skillet and cook at medium heat , covered, for 30 minutes. Stir occasionally. Add remaining ingredients and simmer, covered for about 1 1/2 hours. Remove the scum from the top as it rises to the surface. Cool quickly and check seasoning. Strain and return to the refrigerator. Use within two days or freeze for later use.

Brodo di vitello

HOMEMADE VEAL STOCK

Ingredients

3 veal shank bones

1 white onion, peeled
   and quartered

2 medium carrots peeled

4 celery stalks

2 peeled cloves garlic

Flat leaf parsley stems

3 fresh thyme sprigs

Salt and black pepper

Method
Roast the veal bones for 40 minutes in a preheated 350 degree Fahrenheit oven. deglaze the pan with a little boiling water, scraping up any caramelized juices from the bottom. Put the bones, the roasting juices, and all the other ingredients except salt into a large pan, cover with 3 quarts of cold water and bring to a boil skimming off any scum as it comes to the surface. Lower the heat and simmer gently for up to 2 hours. Strain, season with salt and cool.

Pasta semolina

SEMOLINA PASTA

Ingredients

1 pound semolina flour

1 pound high gluten flour

1/4 cup olive oil

1 cup cold water

4 large eggs

1 tablespoon salt

Method
In an electric mixer using the dough hook, mix the semolina flour, high gluten flour and salt together. Add the olive oil, water and eggs and mix until the dough just comes together. Turn out the dough onto a floured work surface and knead the dough for 2 to 3 minutes. Let the dough rest for at least 1 hour before rolling out

ACKNOWLEDGEMENTS

I would like to thank the special gifted staff of JAMES AT THE MILL Restaurant whose genuine care for making people happy has always been the secret of our success and for allowing me the freedom to explore and create. For their direct involvement in "A Tuscan Seduction", I would like to thank Lori McLeod, Nathan Jendesky, Kingpin, Jesus Chaves, Kelly Ledding, Melecio Velasco, Don Ray, Lyle James and our General Manager Richard Ayson and Lyle.

Special thanks to my mentors, Guy Savoy, David Burke, Don Pintabona, and Mark Miller for allowing me to discover the world of creative cuisine by cooking in their kitchens.
I also owe a great deal of gratitude to Sir Richard and Ruth Rogers for the kindness they extended to me while working in their wonderful RIVER CAFE in London. Their Chef, Rose Gray, creates the finest Tuscan Cuisine in the world, outside of Italy. She was generous with her instruction and instilled in me the respect and appreciation for the food of Tuscany. My time with her laid the foundation for this cookbook.

Lastly, I would like to thank my friend and professor, Giuliano Gargani, for the hours of discussion about the arts and of the food of Tuscany. I treasure the time I spent with him in his Florentine Trattoria, GARGA. His intellect and artistry live with me.

MJ

My thanks to a wonderful staff for giving me the time off to pursue my rather eclectic interests. Thank you to Im Hun Bae, Patty Smith, and Tonya Immel for sailing my personal boat and to Lorene Lambeth Husmann (Mom), Nancy Marshall, John Delap, Phyllis Sizemore, and Wes Osburn for keeping the fleet sailing in the right direction.

During these final moments of getting the book off to press, I would like to thank Wendy Lott and Angela Lowry. I would also like to thank Lee Holt of Collier's Photo and Digital for their skill in making us look good.

JL

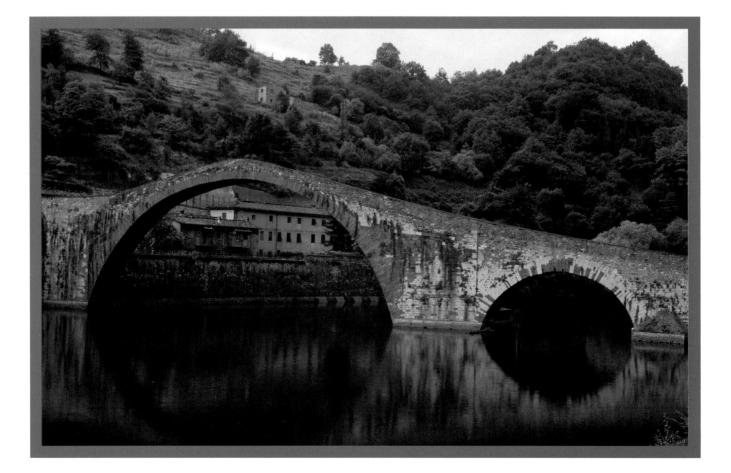

E D I B L E   F L O W E R S

The first time I remember having flowers served with food was a decade ago in Florence. The chef, Giuliano Gargani, used rose petals to garnish the dish of roasted veal. The many colored flowers had been torn into confetti. I had entered a new world of beauty and delight. Not only do contemporary Italians enjoy the beauty and flavor of flowers, the ancient Romans also enjoyed the custom. Their favorite flower was from the Caper plant. Because the flower lasted such a short time they later developed a method of preserving the Caper Berry in Olive Oil. Today flowers are preserved by drying and coating the petals with egg white and sugar crystals.

We love the bounty of edible flowers that grow in the Ozarks and use them throughout the summer months in our restaurant and at home. We have used the "Tuscan Tradition" in this cookbook. The most illustrated is the Zucchini Blossom (page 99, 100). Other edible flowers that are common in America are the Rose (pages 115 and 127), the Pansy (page 23), the Red Bud (page 107), Tulips (95) Johnny Jump Ups and Nasturtiums (page 19). We have illustrated some of our favorite edible flowers below. Remember to eat only organically grown flowers. Also be sure to remove the stamen on large flowers. Eat in moderation and make sure they are edible by using only the ones we have recommended.

When you travel to Florence, walk along the north side of the Arno River west of the Ponte Vecchio. You will see the many beautiful roses at the water's edge that are the flowers of Giuliano Gargani. On very special days you might see him in a white robe, tending his roses. Then for a perfect evening, go to his restaurant, Garga, and dine on incredible food adorned with his flowers.

SUNFLOWER (HELIANTHUS ANNUUS)   NASTURTIUM (TROPAEOLUM MAJUS)   YUCCA (YUCCA FILAMENTOSA)
HIBISCUS (HIBISKOS MALLOW)   TULIP (TULIPA)   PANSY (VIOLA X WITTROCKIANA)
HOLLYHOCK (ALCEA ROSEA)   DAYLILY (HEMEROCALLIS FULVA)   ROSE (ROSA)

EAT ONLY ORGANICALLY GROWN FLOWERS/REMOVE STAMENS. EAT IN MODERATION

P H O T O G R A P H Y   I N D E X

BIBLIOGRAPHY

2 • Sondheim, Steven, and Rogers, Richard, "Take the Moment" from *Do I Hear a Waltz*, Broadway Musical, New York, NY, © 1965

14 • Rice, Ann, *Interview with a Vampire*, New York, NY, Alfred A. Knoph, 1999, original © 1976

18 • Golden, Arthur, *Memoirs of a Geisha*, New York, NY, Alfred A.Knoph, 1999, original © 1997

22 • Carroll, Lewis, *Through the Looking Glass*, NY, NY, New American Library, June, 1995, original print 1877

26 • Fitzgerald, F. Scott, *The Great Gatsby*, New York, NY, Scribner, 1995, original © 1929

30 • Heller, Joseph, *Catch 22*, New York, NY, Simon and Schuster, 1989, original © 1961

34 • "Song of Songs", from *The Holy Bible / The Old Testament*

38 • L'Amour, Louis, *The Walking Drum*, New York, NY, Bantam Doubleday Dell Publishing Group, © 1985

47 • Flaubert, Gustave, *Madame Bovary*, New York, NY, Barnes and Noble Classics, 1993, original print 1857

50 • Harris, Thomas, *Hannibal*, New York, NY, Delacorte Press, Random House, Incorporated, © 1999

54 • De Sade, Marquis, translated by Austryn Wainhouse, *Justine*, NY, NY, Grove Press, 1990, original print 1780

58 • Michelangelo, translated by Greighton Gilbert, *Unfinished Sonnet*, Princeton, NJ, Princeton University Press, 1980, original print 1507

62 • Poe, Edgar Allan, "For Annie", from *The Complete Tales and Poems of Edgar Allan Poe*, New York, NY, Barnes and Noble Books, 1994, original print 1849

70 • Hugo, Victor, T*he Hunchback of Notre Dame*, NY, NY, Barnes and Noble Books, 1996, original print 1831

74 • Updike, John, *In the Beauty of the Lillies*, New York, NY, Alfred A. Knoph, Publishing, 1996, original © 1984

78 • Hemingway, Ernest, *A Farewell to Arms*, New York, NY, Simon and Schuster, June, 1995, original © 1929

82 • Williams, Tennessee, *The Field of Blue Lillies*, New York, NY, New Directions Pub. Corp., 1985, original © 1939

86 • Cervantes, Miguel de Saavedra, translated by J.M. Cohen, *Don Quixote*, New York, NY, Barnes and Noble, 1999, original print 1614

90 • Sendak, Maurice, *Where the Wild Things Are*, New York, NY, Harper Collins Pub., Inc., 1998, original © 1963

94 • Pasternak, Boris, *Doctor Zhivago*, New York, NY, Everymans Library, 1991, original © 1958

98 • Buckley Jr, William F., *The Story of Henry Todd*, Nashville, TN, Cumberland House, Sept., 1996, original © 1984

102 • Lawrence, D.H., *Lady Chatterly's Lover*, New York, NY, Modern Library, 1993, original © 1928

106 • Suess, Doctor, *Oh, the Places You'll Go.* New York, NY, Random House, January, © 1990

110 • Warhol, Andy, *The Philosophy of Andy Warhol: A to B and Back Again*, New York, NY, Harcourt Brace and Company, February, © 1977

114 • Rand, Ayn, *The Fountainhead*, New York, NY, Simon and Schuster, 2000, original © 1943

118 • Rancati, Gino, *Ferrari, A Memory*, Osciola, WI, Motorbooks Inter. Pub. and Wholesalers, 1989, orig. © 1976

142 • McCartney, Paul, and Lennon, John, "The End" from *Beatles: Abbey Road,* © 1969

ITALIAN INDEX

INDEX

"And in the end
the love you take
is equal to
the love you make."

JOHN LENNON and PAUL MCCARTNEY
from THE END. 1969